Reaching Every Child

HOW TO MEET STUDENT NEEDS

Concordia Publishing House Saint Louis

3558 S. Jefferson Ave., St. Louis, MO 63118-3968

1-800-325-3040 • www.cph.org

Text of readings by Dave Andrus, Dave Ebeling, Amanda Geidel, Jim Gimbel, Rachel Hoyer, Lisa Krenz, Loren Sheppard, Anita Reith Stohs, and Karen Wittmayer.

Questions by Kaellyn Marrs and Mark S. Sengele

Editors: Tom Nummela and Mark S. Sengele

Cover art: iStock/Thinkstock

Manufactured in the United States of America.

1 2 3 4 5 6 7 8 9 10 24 23 22 21 20 19 18 17 16 15

Table of Contents

Introduction: A Theological Perspective

God's inclusive plan is for all who believe. Since the goal for inclusion in the Sunday School classroom is to nurture a child's relationship with Christ, it is important to ask: Who is Jesus Christ?

Who Is Christ?

Christian theology teaches that Jesus is the Second Person of the triune God, begotten of the Father from eternity. Christ took on human flesh and characteristics from the moment of conception, which He still carries in eternity. Jesus is like us in every way, yet without sin (Hebrews 2:17; 4:15), since He did not inherit original sin. He was and is both fully God and fully human, and we cannot separate His divinity from His humanity. Yet we know that as a human being who possessed divine majesty and power, He did not always use that power while He lived among us. He ate, slept, walked, and talked. Sometimes, however, He *did* use the divine power He possessed, as when He walked on water, fed the multitudes, raised the dead, or healed people who lived with a myriad of physical disabilities.

As true God, Jesus knew all things, including the thoughts of the Pharisees who conspired against Him. In His resurrected body, Jesus is now present and reigning in heaven; present and reigning in and beyond all created places, things, and persons; and uniquely present and reigning in the hearts of all believers. Moreover, His body and blood are really present in Communion with the bread and wine of the Lord's Supper.

Jesus could passionately confront the Pharisees, Sadducees, and the money changers in the temple, but He also loved them all, working to help them understand His purpose, turning critics into Christians. He was able, at twelve, to teach the most learned religious teachers of His day, yet He indicates that faith is simple enough that little children can "believe in Me" (Matthew 18:6).

Faith in Christ

How much of Christ must we know and understand in order to be saved? We are called to "believe in the Lord Jesus, and . . . be saved" (Acts 16:31)—not believe *about* (know content), but believe *in* (have a faith relationship with Jesus the Savior).

Christology, the study of Christ, is a worthy endeavor. Learning *theology* leads to *doxology*—praise. However, it is comforting to know that the Holy Spirit works saving faith in a child with a belief or trust that is as small as "a grain of mustard seed" (Matthew 17:20). That faith continues to grow throughout a lifetime.

You may not be able to educate all your students in the full contents of Christology. But you can continue to share the full spectrum of faith, including the simple truth that Jesus died for all, and that, by believing, we "have life in His name" (John 20:31). Sharing the broad but simple truths of Christ and Christianity is the core of including everyone.

How could I use this resource?

Use the articles individually or in a group.

Study one article at a time, or do a few related ones together.

Discuss or ponder the opening thought.

Consider how the article impacts teaching the Christian faith.

Talk about how the content applies to your setting.

And they shall be My people, and I will be their God. I will give them one heart and one way, that they may fear Me forever, for their own good and the good of their children after them.
Jeremiah 32:38–39

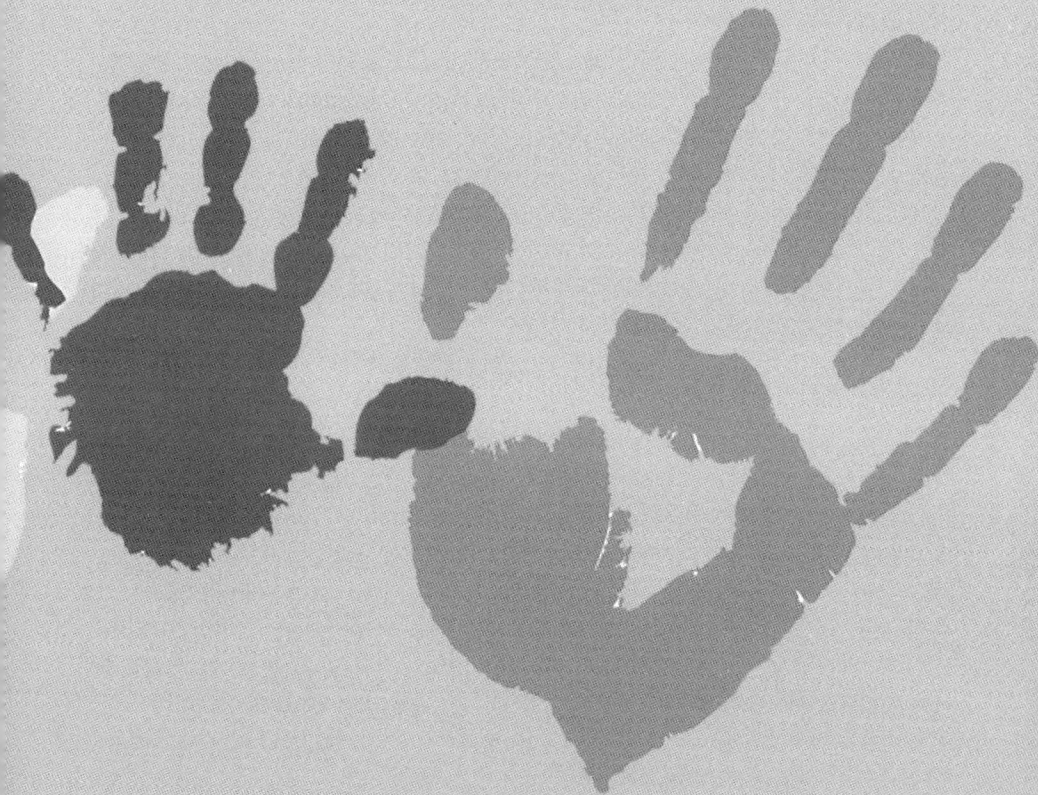

Section 1

Student Needs—Then and Now

OPENING THOUGHT

What are some ways our society has changed in the past decades?

Times, and Teaching, Have Changed

Lisa Krenz

Review

Even though it doesn't seem like very long ago, so much about our world has changed in the past forty years. Internet, DVDs, and smart phones are just a drop in the bucket of changes during these swiftly passing few decades. But more important than the ever-expanding world of new technology and scientific advances is a change in the way society accepts people who are different from the majority. Civil rights legislation paved the way for special education legislation in the 1970s and the Americans with Disabilities Act in the early 1990s.

Out of Sight in the Past

If I had been born with a mental or physical disability, my parents would have been expected and encouraged to hide me at home or commit me to an institution. Parents who chose instead to raise their "handicapped" child at home might have had their child turned away by the public schools. I was not born with a disability, and I attended schools that were void of children who functioned differently than I. I missed something. Children with disabilities were regulated to special schools or isolated classrooms. Since these terms had not even been coined, children with learning disabilities or attention deficit disorder struggled in silence and got no help beyond what the creative teacher could do alone.

Churches were not much different. In those churches where children with disabilities were welcomed, they were typically segregated, placed in classes apart from everyone else.

A Common Sight Today

The world has changed since I pinned on my first Sunday School pin. Children today regularly have classmates—both in school and in Sunday School—with a wide variety of special needs. Children with special needs are frequently seen in all locations and activities, including advertising or television. Curriculum has changed as well, reflecting our increased knowledge of meeting the needs of all learners through a variety of learning strategies.

Today, in our country, children with disabilities are provided with an appropriate education, learning alongside other children their age whenever possible. Access to buildings, bathrooms, telecommunications, and job opportunities are just a few of the guarantees provided by law to people with disabilities.

What is your congregation's approach to children with special needs? We need to have more than just accessible buildings and bathrooms. We need accessible hearts and open minds. We need to look for the ways we can make things work instead of the reasons why things won't work for students with special needs. Many Sunday Schools employ team teaching and teaching aides to assist with students with special needs. All of our children, regardless of ability, are better off for these kinds of changes in Sunday School.

THINK ABOUT

- How does your congregation approach children with special needs and their families?
- What does it mean to have accessible hearts and open minds?

OPENING THOUGHT

Are children growing up today different than the children of previous generations? Why or why not?

Kids Today . . .

Lisa Krenz

Review

"Kids today, humph! Life's not like it was when I was young." We've all heard that lament. And it's true! The lives of children today are different from those of previous generations—more media options, less clear lines of authority, more day care, less time just to be kids, and on and on. Recent studies show that girls are reaching puberty at an earlier age. The incidence of special needs like attention deficit disorder, learning disabilities, and autism is on the rise. It seems the world of child development gets more complex all the time.

But let's look at the flip side of the coin. Much is still the same about children.

They are still children.

While children may be exposed to more, we must not be fooled into thinking that they are able to process the input or can function on the same level as adults. While today's children may appear to be more mature physically, they can't think on a true abstract level until they are at least 11 years old. A child with exceptional learning needs may not achieve abstract thinking until an even older age.

How children learn remains the same.

Children still learn best when they use all their senses. They still need to touch things, experiment with the world around them, and experience things firsthand. The human brain still loves music, rhythm, and rhyme. Children still don't learn things the first time.

Since much of Christian education is abstract, children still need guided experiences to move from the concrete to the abstract, starting with the known and moving to the unknown. We can't expect young children to make cognitive jumps. When we ask students to think and learn beyond their stage of development, we invite discipline problems or diminished learning.

How good were the good old days?

Perhaps the "good old days" weren't always so good. The model students—sitting quietly with hands folded in rows of desks—if they ever existed, may not have learned much. Yes, kids today are different in some ways, and so are we. Yet some things remain the same. Children still need to know this Jesus who loves them and died and rose again for their salvation. As a favorite children's song reminds us: "Jesus loves the little children, All the children of the world." By God's grace, may that never change!

THINK ABOUT

- How has childhood changed in recent years? How has it remained the same?
- How can you teach students in ways that use all their senses?
- What are some concepts your students may need help understanding?

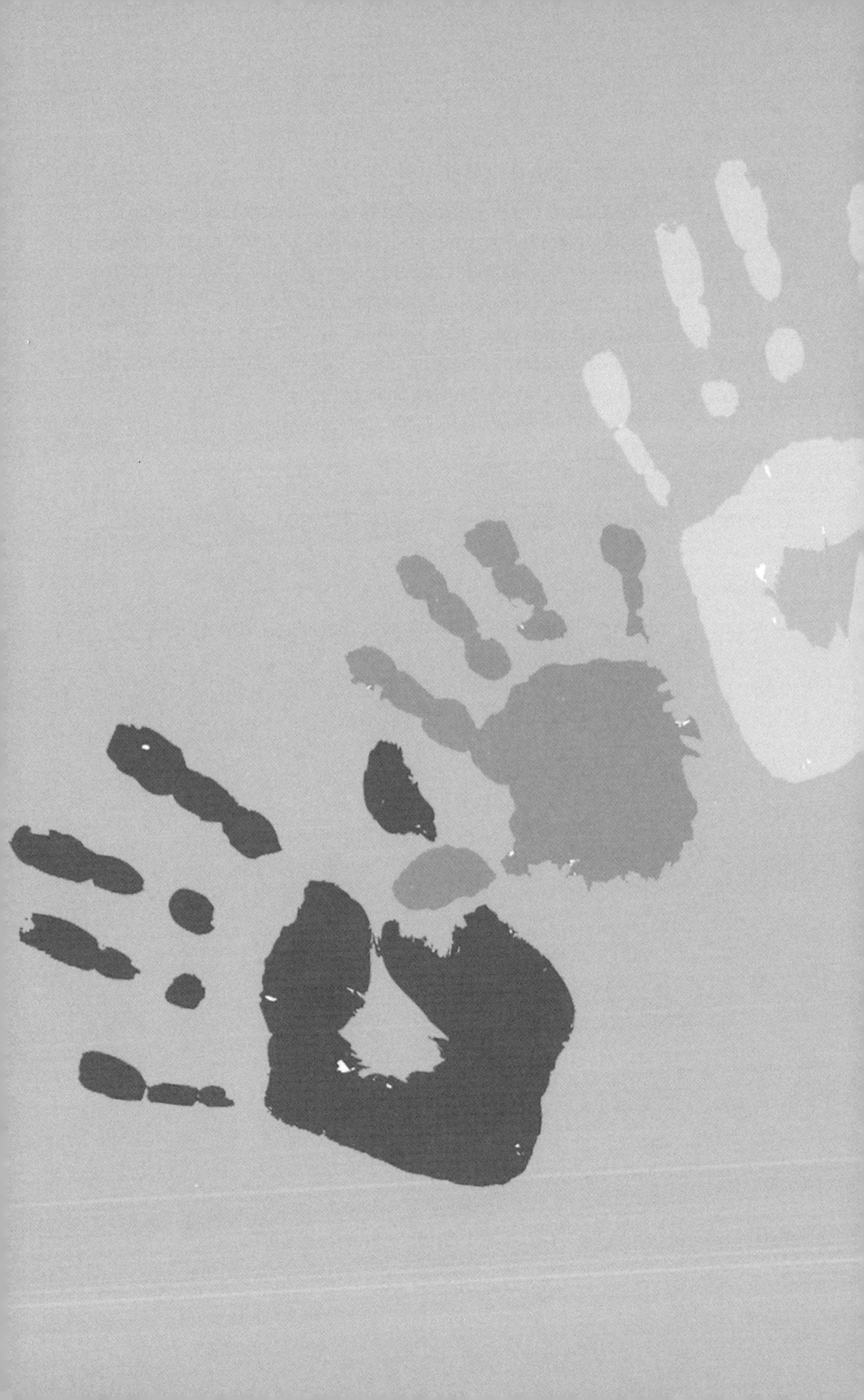

Give instruction to a wise man, and he will be still wiser; teach a righteous man, and he will increase in learning.
Proverbs 9:9

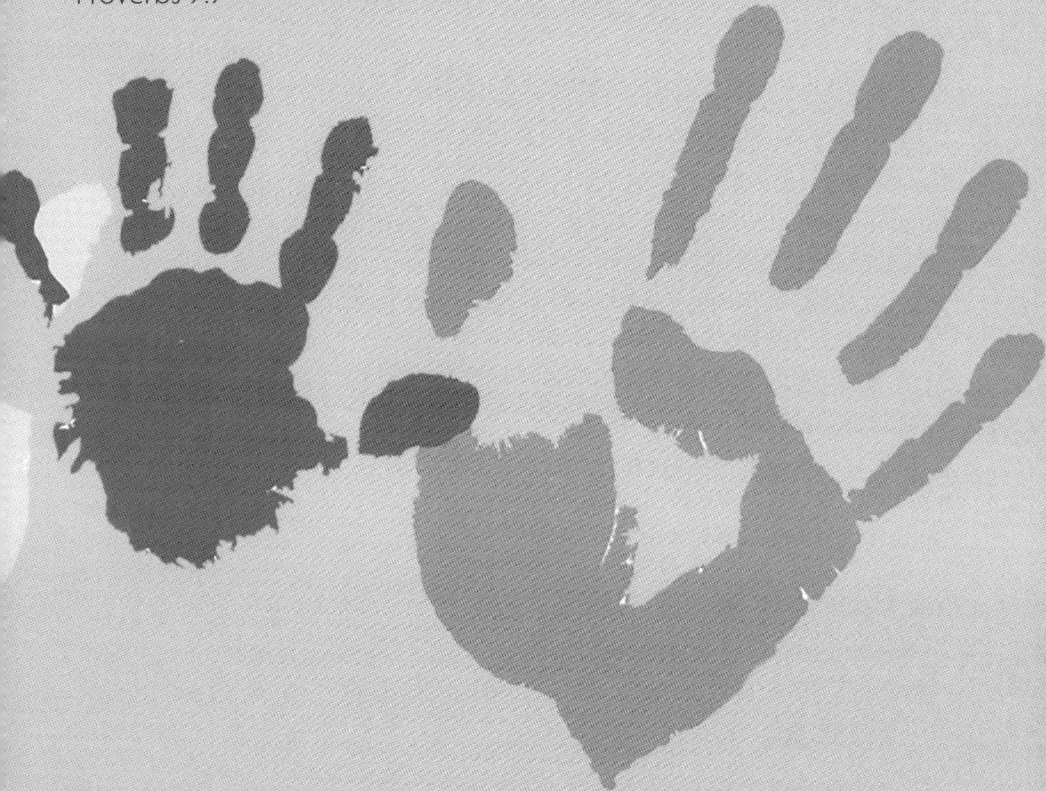

Section 2
What Psychologists Say

OPENING THOUGHT

Think about different ways children grow.

Meeting Children's Needs

Rachel Hoyer

Review

"Sir, we wish to see Jesus" (John 12:21).

Those simple words from Scripture are engraved on the pulpit in the church where I grew up. My Sunday School class saw them as we toured the empty sanctuary. We each got to stand in the pulpit to see from the pastor's point of view. The pastor told us he read that inscription before he delivered each sermon. It reminded him that his job was to help those sitting before him see Jesus so they, in turn, could help the world beyond the pew see Jesus too.

As Sunday School teachers, that's one of our biggest jobs—to help the children placed in our care for an hour each week see Jesus. We do that by teaching the lesson for the day, singing songs, and helping the children create crafts. We also do that by meeting children where they are developmentally.

See How the Children Grow

The children we serve have a range of needs—spiritual, physical, and emotional. There are five basic ways children develop.

1. **Physically:** The child's body changes and motor skills develop.
2. **Emotionally:** The child learns to understand and manage emotions.
3. **Intellectually:** The child learns to think independently and to reason.
4. **Socially:** The child learns to work and play with others.
5. **Spiritually:** The child's faith develops and moves from head to heart.

At any given time, children are growing in at least one of these areas. We have no way of knowing what happens daily in the homes of the children we teach. We can make a pretty good guess about whether a child is being fed spiritually at home or whether Sunday School is the only spiritual food the child gets all week. We can make sure Sunday School offers a buffet of activities that will feed children what they need.

Children's needs change as they grow. While each child goes through basically the same stages and grows in all five areas listed above, they won't happen at the same time or in the same way. Knowing the general needs of an age group, even as we remember that each child is unique, will equip us to teach God's Word to each child in our care.

Basic Levels of Child Development

Ages 4 to 6

Biggest Needs

- Structure, routine, organization, stability
- Adults who offer guidance and encouragement

Key Factors

- Short attention spans
- Egocentric—"It's all about me!"
- Fine- and gross-motor skills are still developing.
- Not results oriented—this group likes to build and destroy just for fun. The finished product isn't the goal.

What You Can Do

- Keep your class structured and moving. Shorter segments will keep their attention.
- Show them unconditional love and encouragement. Help them feel the love of Jesus in your classroom.
- Be engaged. If you are having fun, they will too.

Ages 7 to 9

Biggest Needs

- Structure being part of a group, having choices
- Adults who encourage them to try new things and recognize and acknowledge their accomplishments

Key Factors

- Longer attention spans
- Need help with nuances and seeing other viewpoints
- Problem solving and mysteries are fun.

What You Can Do

- This age still needs a lot of structure. Their attention span is longer, so you can stretch an activity to twenty or thirty minutes.
- This group tends to think in absolutes. Help them learn to settle differences by looking at the other person's point of view.
- Model forgiveness and remind them of God's grace.
- Introduce small outreach projects such as writing letters to soldiers overseas or inviting unchurched friends to Sunday School to help this group think beyond themselves.

Ages 10 to 13

Biggest Needs

- Independence, a sense of responsibility, accountability
- Adults who provide a safe environment for examining the world in which we live, who listen, and who make them feel safe and loved

Key Factors

- More abstract thinking
- Self-conscious about body and appearance
- Occasional moodiness (regardless of gender)

What You Can Do

- Provide a secure environment where these tweens (those between childhood and teenage years; preteen) feel safe sharing thoughts and feelings with one another and with you.
- Develop independence and responsibility by having them lead devotions for class, create mission projects, or help tell Bible stories to preschoolers.
- Allow them flexibility.
- Remind them that they are precious children of God, no matter how old they get.

It's easy to see that our students are still growing physically each year; it's easy to forget that they are growing emotionally as well. Brain research from the National Institute of Mental Health shows that a child's brain—specifically the frontal lobe, responsible for planning, impulse control, and reasoning—continues to develop into the early twenties. We can better meet their needs if we spend some time focusing on that less-obvious mental growth and looking at the whole child instead of an isolated skill or behavior.

Letting the Child Help Us Learn

In the bathroom at a doctor's office, my preschooler asked, "Mommy, do doctors have to go to the bathroom?" When I assured him they did, he asked, "What about restaurant people? Do they have to go too?" This was a revelation to him—and to me. I assumed he knew that all people use the restroom, regardless of their occupation. I forgot that his brain isn't there yet. He's still at the stage where if he doesn't see it happen, it may not happen.

I had to change the way I was thinking about my son and reevaluate where he is in his brain development. I learned not to take his developmental stage for granted. As teachers, we may need to change the way we look at and think about the children in our classrooms.

Let's say you give your second graders scissors, glue, and quick instructions for a craft project. Halfway through the allotted time, Sierra has her papers cut and arranged correctly and is beginning to glue them together according to instructions. Caleb, on the other hand, is nowhere near done cutting, and he isn't cutting in straight lines. There's no way he'll finish. Why can't Caleb be like Sierra? Is Caleb lazy? not paying attention? just a boy? No, no, and no.

While it would be nice for all children to mature at the same time and on the same schedule, that's not how it works. What are things Caleb can do well? He sings beautifully. He's a good friend. Right now, Caleb's body and brain may be focused on emotional skills such as empathy and social awareness. His body may be putting the physical skill of cutting on the back burner for the moment. Sierra's body and brain have been hard at work on fine-motor skills and focusing. It could be that Sierra's brain and body aren't quite ready to sing a song in tune or show empathy to those around her.

Will Sierra and Caleb ultimately gain all those skills? Yes, we certainly hope so. But until they do, it's our job to meet them where they are—individually—on the developmental continuum and to help them see Jesus in their lives.

THINK ABOUT

- Think about the students in your classroom. Where do some of them fall on the developmental continuum?
- What can you do to meet them where they are and help them grow?
- How can knowing how your students are developing help you teach them about Jesus?

OPENING THOUGHT

As you read, think about ways that you are smart.

How Your Learners Are Smart

Dave Ebeling

Review

A New Question

"How smart is this child?" teachers and parents are likely to ask. We want to know a number, an IQ score, from a paper-and-pencil test. However, God created everyone with many kinds of intelligence—ways they are smart. So we might ask instead, "How is this child smart?"

Multiple Intelligences Theory

To answer that question, we can look at the work of Harvard researcher Dr. Howard Gardner. In his book, *Frames of Mind,* Gardner proposes that all humans are smart, but we're smart in different ways. He identifies multiple ways people are intelligent, giving us a tool to think about learners in an alternative way.

Gardner and other proponents now identify at least eight different ways a learner can be intelligent, which Gardner calls "Multiple Intelligences" (MI). Almost all humans have intelligences in all eight ways. We all have multiple intelligences. It is also true that most humans excel or have a preference for one or more intelligence areas. We tend to learn better if the instruction is in the context of one or more of our preferred intelligences.

Gardner's theory is not without its critics, who see no empirical data for it and prefer to see his intelligences as abilities—all parts of one intelligence. Whether one fully accepts the theory, however, many educators observe these preferences in learning style in their classrooms and find the concepts useful for reaching all kinds of learners.

Multiple Intelligences

Check out these thumbnail sketches of the eight categories of Multiple Intelligences proposed by Howard Gardner. There are hundreds of ways to demonstrate each kind of intelligence. Those listed are simply a few examples of each.

1. Linguistic/Verbal Intelligence

These learners are skilled in and have a passion for words. We might call them "Word Smart."

- Children in class are good readers, like to write, enjoy conversation, and have a large vocabulary.
- Adults may choose to work as reporters, authors, poets, bloggers, pastors, or teachers.

2. Logical/Mathematical Intelligence

These learners are skilled in and have a passion for numbers, logic, and inductive and deductive reasoning. We might call them "Math Smart."

- Children in class like puzzles, want to know why things work, are problem solvers, and find math easy.
- Adults may choose to work as accountants, physicians, engineers, clerks, or statisticians.

3. Spatial/Visual Intelligence

These learners are skilled in and have a passion for art, color, or design. We might call them "Art Smart."

- Children in class enjoy cartooning, illustrating, or just doodling in the margins. Their imaginations are vivid.
- Adults may choose to work as graphic artists, musicians, clothing or interior designers, or architects.

4. Musical/Rhythmic Intelligence

These learners are skilled in and have a passion for music. We might call them "Music Smart."

- Children in class can tap out the beat to music, will hum along, and ask to sing or play instruments.

- Adults may choose to attend concerts, listen to music, play an instrument as a hobby or profession, compose music, or teach music.

5. Bodily/Kinesthetic Intelligence

These learners are skilled in and have a passion for physical activity. We might call them "Body Smart."

- Children in class probably are physically coordinated and enjoy active games, running, and exercise.
- Adults likely will stay physically active, participate in runs/walks, join a team, bicycle, dance, and swim. They may find careers in athletics, acting, building, or the military.

6. Naturalistic Intelligence

These learners are skilled in and have a passion for nature and the outdoors. We might call them "Nature Smart."

- Children in class often are attracted to plants and animals and prefer being outdoors, where they can investigate bugs or study the stars.
- Adults likely will be advocates of their natural surroundings, value the environment, and are likely to have pets. They may work in park or zoo management or farming.

7. Intrapersonal Intelligence

These learners are skilled in and have a passion for deep thinking and introspection. We might call them "Self Smart."

- Children in class may be less verbal, ask deep questions, and probe details of answers. They are keenly aware of their own feelings, strengths, ideas, and beliefs.

8. Interpersonal Intelligence

These learners are skilled in and have a passion for people and the feelings, moods, and motives of others. We might call them "People Smart."

- Children in class interact easily with other children and adults.
- Adults might be politicians or the organizers of the next church fellowship. They offer to help others resolve conflict and like to work and be with other people.

MI in Sunday School

Our Sunday School classrooms have children representing strengths in most or all eight intelligence areas. MI proponents observe that children will be more motivated and learn faster if the instruction allows them to learn from one of their preferred intelligence strengths.

As an example, consider a Sunday morning when your story for the day is the account of Zacchaeus. Certainly we want every child to see Jesus in this story. We want them to recognize that He sought out Zacchaeus, confronted him with his sins, and shared with him the Good News of forgiveness. We want to help the children see that Zacchaeus became a changed man after meeting Jesus and accepting His forgiveness—indeed, the Bible describes what he did differently after receiving forgiveness. We want the children to be changed too.

In teaching that story using the MI concepts, the teacher would choose activities that specifically interest children who are intelligent in different, multiple ways. Here are several examples of what a teacher might do when teaching about Zacchaeus:

For **Word Smart** learners: Read the story from different translations. Rewrite the story as a dramatic reading.

For **Math Smart** learners: Calculate how much Zacchaeus would have repaid if he had overcharged different amounts of taxes.

For **Art Smart** learners: Use paper or textiles to design and create a sycamore tree inside your classroom space, perhaps around a stepladder.

For **Music Smart** learners: Sing "Zacchaeus Was a Wee Little Man." Use rhythm instruments if available.

For **Body Smart** learners: Have children "pretend climb" a tree, using large muscles.

For **Nature Smart** learners: Learn about the sycamore tree. Was it common in Bible lands? What made it easy for Zacchaeus to climb?

For **Self Smart** learners: Challenge learners to express what Zacchaeus may be thinking upon hearing Jesus say, "Zacchaeus, you come down. I'm going to your house today."

For **People Smart** learners: Discuss: "Picture yourselves near the tree when Jesus talked to Zacchaeus. What might they have said to each other?"

Try MI in Four Simple Steps

1. Become familiar with the eight kinds of intelligences.

2. Know your students well enough to identify one or two of the Multiple Intelligences that seem to be their personal strengths.

3. Look at the lesson activities and teaching ideas in your teacher guide. Choose those activities that match your learners' preferences.

4. Don't be concerned that you cover all eight of the Multiple Intelligences in every lesson.

THINK ABOUT

- In which areas of intelligence do I excel?
- In which areas of intelligence do my students excel?
- I can incorporate Multiple Intelligences into my next lesson by . . .

OPENING THOUGHT

What abstract concepts are common in the Sunday School lessons I teach?

FACT Development, FAITH Development

Lisa Krenz

Review

When you go to college to become a teacher, you learn about a fellow named Piaget and his theory of cognitive development. It's good stuff. A great deal of how we understand and educate children is based on his theory, and it is worthy of deeper study as you think about your own teaching.

A brief overview of Piaget shows us that school-aged children generally fall into three stages of development: Preoperational (ages 2–7) and Concrete Operations (ages 7–11), with older children beginning to reach the third stage of Formal Operations (age 11+). Children in the Preoperational stage are mastering symbolic thinking, expressing concepts in proper syntax and grammar, developing conversational skills, and have a strong sense of imagination and intuition. Children in the Concrete Operational stage are learning, just as the name implies, in very concrete ways. They are beginning to understand abstract ideas like time and space but only as they are attached to concrete experiences. After age 11, children begin to work in the Formal Operations stage of abstract thinking, but it's not a perfectly sequential ladder. Students typically go back and forth between stages. Very often, children may be able to think abstractly in one conceptual area but not another.

Potential Delays

It's not uncommon for children with special needs to be delayed as they work their way through these stages. This means teachers need to present material and ask for responses in a more concrete, less abstract, way. Often, this benefits all the concrete thinkers in the group, usually a majority of the class. Think of how many times you hear an adult say they get more out of the children's sermon because it's a concrete explanation of an abstract idea.

On the flip side of this topic, however, consider that cognitive development (making meaning of the world) and faith development are not quite the same set of skills. Faith development is a much broader activity than cognitive development alone. Obviously, teachers need to present lessons in an age-appropriate and cognition-appropriate manner, but it's imperative that we leave room for the Holy Spirit.

Fact Development ≠ Faith Development

At first glance, faith is a pretty abstract concept, and yet children who struggle with other abstract concepts (or can't grasp them at all) have faith. A child's fact development might be delayed. They may struggle to memorize Bible verses, complete worksheets, listen attentively, or do sermon notes. These skills are not, however, a measure of faith development. For a student with special needs, these cognitive skills may lag behind their same-aged peers, but rest assured; this doesn't mean the Holy Spirit isn't doing mighty work in their hearts, developing a faith beyond measure.

THINK ABOUT

- Faith development is different than fact development because . . .
- Which stages of development do my students fall into? Preoperational? Concrete? Formal?
- Which of my students could benefit from more concrete teaching?

Now they were bringing even infants to Him that He might touch them. And when the disciples saw it, they rebuked them. But Jesus called them to Him saying, "Let the children come to Me, and do not hinder them, for to such belongs the kingdom of God."

Luke 18:15–16

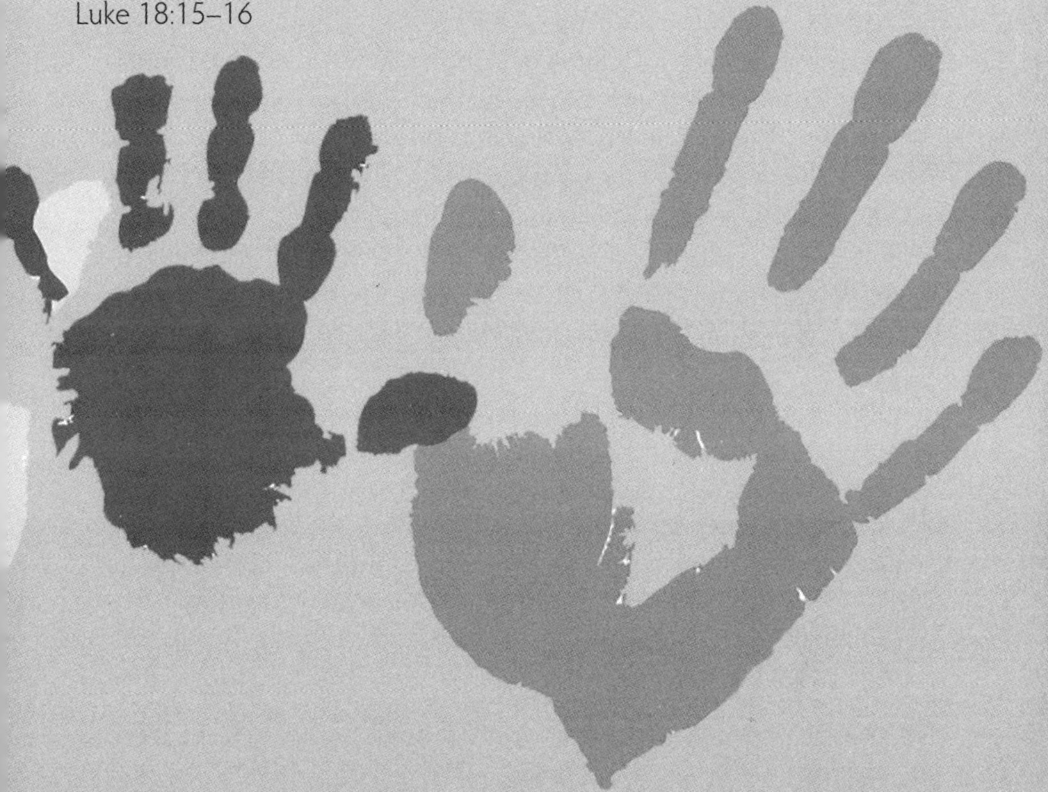

Section 3

Where to Begin

OPENING THOUGHT

What is your church currently doing to include children with special needs?

Building Blocks of Faith: Meeting Learning Needs

Lisa Krenz

Review

Why do parents send their children to Sunday School? There are undoubtedly many reasons. Parents want their children to learn about Jesus and His love for them. Parents want their children to be part of a community of faith and have fellowship with other believers, both children and adults. Parents want their children to gain Bible knowledge that will support their faith now and in the future. Parents want their children to learn about loving others as God has loved them. As Christian parents and teachers, these responses sound obvious and simple. We send our children to Sunday School with the hopes of providing our children with some building blocks of faith.

Parents of children with special needs send their children to Sunday School for the very same reasons. They want to provide them with those same building blocks of faith. They, too, want their children to know Jesus and to gain Bible knowledge that provides the Word of life. They, too, want their children to be part of a community of faith and fellowship with the other Christians. They, too, want their children to learn to love others as God has loved them. All children have the same need to know Jesus as their Savior. This is not a special need—it is a universal need!

That seems obvious. In reality, matters may not be that simple. What does it look like to include children with special needs in your Sunday School program? How can the gifted students remain challenged? How do you accommodate for everyone's different needs? You may be thinking, "We aren't special education teachers. We don't know enough. I've never dealt with children with these special needs. I'm frightened that I'll do the wrong thing." These are very common and understandable concerns. Don't let your concerns deter you from opening your Sunday School to children with special needs and their families; instead, let them be the first steps. You will have the awesome chance to witness God's mighty hand at work.

At Cross Lutheran Church in Yorkville, Illinois, Truby Szewczyk (chef-chik) coordinates including children with special needs in their Sunday School. Truby has the wonderful opportunity to pray for specific needs of children and see how God answers those prayers in very real ways right there in their Sunday School. After Truby and others begin with prayer, Truby goes to work and sets up the learning situations for each individual child with special needs. The children have needs that include ADHD, mental impairments, hearing impairments, and learning disabilities. According to Truby, "children with special needs fit right in because [their Sunday School is] so multisensory. All children get a chance to show how they learn best in all their modalities."

A Case Study

The Sunday School program at Cross Lutheran is dominated by music, lots of interactive activities and materials, as well as learning games. This already makes Truby's job easier, because fewer adaptations are needed to accommodate individual children. Each child's situation is considered from an individual perspective. In certain situations, one adult teacher simply cannot attend to such issues while teaching the many children in class. Some children may need teacher's assistants to help them be successful in class. The simple needs that arise, like taking a child to the restroom or preventing behavior problems from escalating, can easily be handled. At Cross Lutheran, even though there may be many children in a particular grade, each grade level is divided into groups of 8–10 children. Due to small class sizes, many kinds of learners easily fit in fine without an extra adult. The teacher knows the students well enough to accommodate for all the different learning differences in the class. The small class size also helps children develop a very close personal connection with their teacher.

Cross Lutheran is also flexible about all children being in class with students their own age. Sometimes it is very appropriate and works out well. Other times it might be more beneficial for a student with special learning needs to be with slightly younger students. When developing the right learning situation for each child, Truby listens closely to parents. She says, "They know their children best." It's obvious that Truby values the insights parents share and appreciates their input about what their children's needs are and how their children learn best.

Faith Building Blocks at Cross Lutheran

Prayer—Truby and all the teachers pray for their students right from the start. She may also ask others who are not part of the Sunday School staff to intercede on behalf of specific children or teachers.

Music—Music is an integral part of their Sunday School program. It benefits children of all ages. Music has long been known to reach people with learning difficulties in a way that other methods could not. Research into learning and brain function shows a strong correlation between music involvement and learning. You can probably remember songs you learned in your childhood, though other details or texts have been long forgotten. Truby also notices how the enthusiasm for music that the students with special needs demonstrate is contagious.

Multisensory activities—There is an old saying, Tell me and I will forget; show me and I will remember; involve me and I will understand. This really holds true in helping children with exceptional learning needs. In learning activities that rely on skills and abilities other than reading and writing, teachers will need to make fewer adaptations for students who have deficits in those skills. This multisensory approach also lends itself well to students who struggle to sit still.

Small groupings of students—Smaller groups make it easier for teachers to know all their students and make adaptations as needed. It also helps facilitate positive fellowship experiences among all students.

Partnership with parents—Parents are their children's first teachers and know what their children need. They generally appreciate being approached tactfully about helping their children learn as easily as possible. Think about each situation as if it was *your* child in class. What questions would you want the teacher to ask you?

Open hearts—There is no set recipe for including children with special needs in your Sunday School. That means that everyone—teachers, parents, and students—needs to be open to a variety of ideas and suggestions. You'll be amazed at how many good ideas you can generate together. When you open your hearts to God and to one another, amazing things can happen! To quote Truby, "There's nothing to be afraid of."

Your Congregation

Just because Truby isn't a member of your congregation doesn't mean that your congregation can't share the building blocks of faith with children with special needs and their families. There is a "Truby" in your Sunday School—perhaps it's you. With prayer, music, multisensory activities, strong partnerships with parents, and open hearts, children with special needs can learn of the Savior's love for them and all children.

THINK ABOUT

Make a list of things that make the Sunday School program described above unique.

- What are some things on that list that you could implement next week?
- What are some things on that list that might take longer than a week to put into place? How can you begin the process?

OPENING THOUGHT

Think about your students: how are they similar? different?

See How They Grow

Amanda Geidel

Review

It is a Saturday morning in August and you pick up the phone just before it goes to voicemail. “Hello?” “Hi, Susan. This is Marv from church. I was hoping you might be willing to teach a Sunday School class this fall. All the materials are here and ready. All you have to do is prepare one simple lesson for each Sunday. Really, the work is almost done for you with this new curriculum. Can the kiddos count on you?”

Your heart tells you that you should do this. Your head tells you there is no way you can fit another activity into your already packed schedule. Your heart wins and you agree, but just for the fall semester. After all, he did say that the new curriculum does most of the work for you. This should be a piece of cake!

The task of teaching Sunday School on a weekly basis can be much more cumbersome than described during that phone call asking for your help. Often, children attend Sunday School irregularly. It may be a challenge for you to get to know them, to learn what they are capable of or find difficult. That hour of time can fly by, or it can seem to last forever. Your purpose for being there is to share God’s love to all who enter that classroom, but the mission can, at times, be frustrating, especially if you lose sight of that purpose. Watching how children grow and being able to see the potential for growth in each one of them just may help you stay true to your mission.

Observe

Children grow and develop at different rates. Each child will vary in size, ability, knowledge, and social skills from others of the same age. Some will actually function a year or two ahead of their peers academically, socially, emotionally, or even spiritually. Others will be a year or two behind in one or more areas. How does a Sunday School teacher identify and teach to the unique level of development of each child? It can generally be done through a process of observation and adjustment. The observant teacher will quickly learn the individual strengths and weaknesses of each child.

Understanding that children are growing in developmental stages in all areas of life and accepting that some are turtles while others are hares will make the Sunday School experience quite comfortable for you and your students.

Adapt

Most teachers make adjustments for a child's unique characteristics. For example, when you notice a student who does not read well, you may adopt a practice of asking for volunteers to read during the Bible study or allowing students to pass up turns to read. If a student is not making friends easily, you may create a seating chart that places this child in closer contact with friendly classmates. If a student is having trouble letting go of Mom's or Dad's hand, you may invite the parent to remain in the room for a time. After a week or two, the child will be ready to let go. It can be helpful to take a few minutes at the end of each class session to make notes about the things you observed that day so that you can use them in your lesson planning.

Multiage Groups

With a little thought, you can adjust for the developmental differences in a multiage group throughout a class session.

- As the children gather, have activities available for a variety of students. Coloring pages and picture books will appeal to nonreaders; puzzle pages and review games will challenge older students.
- In worship, choose a variety of songs and hymns, including some with simple refrains that the youngest children can sing. Structure prayers as litanies with simple responses.
- When the Bible account is presented, older children can read while younger children listen. Or choose an engaging way to present the narrative; all children enjoy hearing a great story!

- Discussion time can be a challenge. Remember a few key principles. Younger children are concrete thinkers; ask them fact-based questions. Students in the middle grades are beginning to develop a sense of chronology; ask them questions that establish the context of the account. Reserve questions that require analytical thinking for older students.
- Use open activities in the application section of a lesson. All children can illustrate how we can live as God's children by drawing pictures, though their pictures will vary greatly in style and detail. Activities requiring writing will not be possible for all children.

Accommodate

The core of your lesson preparation should focus on the developmental level of the majority of the students. From there, you can tweak your lesson to fit the students who are above or below that level, depending on their needs.

After establishing the lesson plan for the core group of students, ask these additional questions.

- Which students will need accommodation—changes in the lesson goals or activities—to participate fully in this lesson?
- What specific changes will be most helpful or necessary? Remember that some students will need to be challenged more in order to keep them involved. Some will need additional support to succeed.

After each session, evaluate the effectiveness of your adaptations. Note what went well and what you will try to do differently next time.

What you do to help each student reach his or her full potential will, of course, depend on the needs of your students. In general, though, there are seven ways that any lesson or activity can be modified to meet the needs of different learners.

1 **Size.** Reduce or increase the size of the activity. If it is memory work, one student may recite the entire Lord's Prayer while another may recite one line of it at a time.

2 **Time.** Increase or decrease the time given to complete an activity. Be sure you have something for the quick finishers to work on when they are done.

3 **Level of Support.** Assign someone—another volunteer or a peer buddy—to work with a student who struggles with the planned activities. Often, you can be the source of extra support.

4 **Input.** Change the way you present the information. Use visual aids and hands-on activities when possible to reach all types of learners.

5 **Output.** Allow students different ways to show what they have learned. This can be done by acting, drawing, speaking, singing, or doing some specific task.

6 **Difficulty.** Change the skill level required of a task or lesson to fit those learners who are at higher or lower achievement levels. A color sheet may be good for one while a crossword puzzle is more pleasing to another.

7 **Participation.** Allow learners to be involved in the activity in different ways. Some can act while others hold up the props or provide sound effects.

Every Sunday School, whether large or small, will face the challenges of adaptation and accommodation. All sets of students vary in developmental progress, and all deserve the opportunity to learn perhaps the most important lesson they'll be taught all week—the message of God's love for us and the gift of His Son as our Savior.

THINK ABOUT

- In your Sunday School classroom, what ages and developmental levels are represented?
- I can differentiate my teaching to fit my students' needs by . . .
- How can you modify your lesson based on size, time, level of support, input, output, difficulty, or participation?

OPENING THOUGHT

What comes to mind when you hear the word *accessible*?

Universal Design for Learning

Lisa Krenz

Review

It's the first warm day of spring and you've dusted off the stroller for a trip through your neighborhood. At the corner, you cruise down the curb cut, across the street, up through the next curb cut, and back up onto the sidewalk. That curb cut makes your excursion much more pleasant, doesn't it? You do not to have to bump the stroller down from the sidewalk and then lift your wheels back up over the curb again. Guess what? Even though you enjoy them, those curb cuts weren't originally intended for you and your stroller. Curb cuts are a result of the 1990 federal legislation called the Americans with Disabilities Act. The purpose of that legislation is accessibility—through and to architecture, communication systems, job opportunities, housing, and more—so people with disabilities can be fully included in their communities.

Barrier Free

Curb cuts are an example of an architectural concept called universal design. The goal of universal design is to make buildings and public places barrier free for all people. However, it is worth noting that many features used in universal design benefit all people, not just those with disabilities.

Educators have taken the concept of universal design and applied it to the classroom. We call it universal design for learning. Its goal is to make curriculum accessible to all learners. Sometimes, traditional ways of presenting material and asking students to respond have been barriers to learning. Those students need a "curb cut" that addresses their individual needs. Sometimes, it's something simple such as providing universally designed scissors or presenting the story in both visual and auditory ways. It may mean offering a variety of ways for students to respond or participate.

Benefitting All

The wonderful thing about attending to universal design for learning is that all students benefit, not just those with specific needs. The adaptations that are necessary for one student are nearly always helpful to many others as well.

Throughout the Gospels, our Lord provided wonderful examples of teaching that meets these principles. He told parables that related to His listeners' lives and experiences. He touched people with His healing hands. He provided food for the hungry that they might even taste His love. Sometimes, He preached to a large crowd; sometimes, He talked to a small group of disciples. He didn't say to Thomas, "What? Where have you been? Weren't you listening all those times?" Instead, He showed him His hands and feet. The ultimate universal design for learning is that our Lord continues to make His love and forgiveness accessible for all of us today through His Word and Sacraments.

THINK ABOUT

- How do you make your church buildings accessible to everyone?
- How do you make your Sunday School classes accessible to everyone?
- A universal design for learning could benefit all students by . . .

OPENING THOUGHT

What are you currently doing to meet the learning needs of your students?

Three Ways to Adapt

Karen Wittmayer

Review

Do you have any students in your class with exceptional learning needs? If so, develop a lesson plan that will encourage and involve them.

As you think about how to meet the individual needs of students in your Sunday School class who learn differently or have unique learning styles, consider making *interventions, accommodations,* or *modifications*. These technical educational terms frequently apply to Sunday School lessons.

Intervention

Interventions are activities designed to resolve problems or fix what a child can't do. They involve the direct teaching of a skill or strategy, such as helping a child sound out an unknown word when he or she reads it orally.

Accommodation

Accommodations are provisions made to help students access information or demonstrate learning. You might allow a student to answer verbally rather than writing answers in a leaflet. You might tell a student what question to answer before you read the story, so he or she knows exactly what to listen for, and then cue the student when his or her answer is coming. Other accommodations include seating a child near you for easy redirection, giving children who need to move the job of errand runner, or providing a student with a buddy to help him or her focus.

Modification

Modifications are changes in what a student is expected to learn or demonstrate. Modifications include shortening memory work and asking a child only fact questions and not application questions.

A guiding question can always be, "What can I do so that all the children in my class will learn at least one fact about the lesson and experience the love of Jesus?" Strive for a plan that meets the needs of each of the children in your class. As you find techniques that work, keep a list that will become a menu of many different interventions, accommodations, and modifications that positively affect a child's ability to learn, remember, and experience the joy of learning God's Word.

Always remember that God promises to be with us through His Word! God has chosen us to be His instrument in teaching His precious children about His abundant love. What a joy!

THINK ABOUT

- I can use intervention in my class by . . .
- I can use accommodation in my class by . . .
- I can use modification in my class by . . .
- What can you do to ensure each child learns a fact about the lesson and experiences God's love?

OPENING THOUGHT

What do you already know about accommodating learners and modifying lessons?

Accommodations and Modifications

Lisa Krenz

Review

Accommodations and modifications are strategies used to improve learning. *Accommodating* means leaving the lesson content the same but making changes in the input or output of material. *Modification* means changing the content or lesson outcomes more significantly. Sometimes these terms are used simultaneously, because they both have to do with changing some part of the lesson. Here are suggestions for ways to accommodate or modify to help learners.

Reading

- Read aloud the story, worksheet, or directions to the student.
- Provide a copy of the story at a different reading level—simplified and with pictures for some, complex language for others.
- Provide text in enlarged font.
- Highlight key direction words or concept words.
- Illustrate written concepts with visual images.
- Allow more time.

Writing

- Use a scribe to write for the student.
- Provide pencil grips.
- Use manipulatives as responders (hold up yes or no cards, move an object from one word to a corresponding picture rather than drawing a line).
- Don't require writing—discuss questions as a group or in pairs.

- Provide models or answers to copy, either on the board for the whole class or on an index card for students to follow individually (copying from the board is sometimes difficult, so an up-close choice may be better).
- Accept spelling, grammar, and syntax errors without correction. (This is Sunday School, not English class.)
- Allow more time.

Behavior

- Allow more time—it's no mistake that time is listed in each category here. For many students, the best gift we can give them is more time: more time to process questions, responses, or your requests. Student frustration can be a leading cause of behavior issues.
- Teach with routines. If students know what you're going to do and when (and that it will remain consistent), you may prevent behavior issues related to dysregulation. Students will have better self-control and can better predict what should or will come next.
- Offer "preferential" seating for proximity control.
- Use a visual cue or private signal arranged prior to class to reduce the need to call the student's name in a negative manner.
- Provide positive and specific reinforcement.
- Vary activities every ten or fifteen minutes.
- Build in movement opportunities.

Just having an extra person in the room to assist is good standard practice. More than anything, continue to share the love of Jesus with *all* students, not just those who read, write, and behave well.

THINK ABOUT

- Identify which suggestions are accommodations and which are modifications.
- What are you already doing to accommodate and modify?
- Which of these suggestions can you implement next week?

Be a Student of Students

Lisa Krenz

OPENING THOUGHT

How do your students like to learn?

Review

Being an effective teacher is more than just knowing your topic well. Knowing information is only half the story. It's also about knowing your students and how they learn. One thing that every Sunday School class has in common is that each child in the class is different, complete with individual strengths, weaknesses, personality traits, interests, and experiences.

Children Differ

Some of your students may have very specific special learning needs that impact your teaching in an obvious way. If a child is not able to communicate easily, you will seek new ways to determine whether that child understands. If a child has a physical disability that affects his or her ability to write, you will find other ways for the student to participate. If a child has a visual or hearing impairment, you will alter your teaching to accommodate those sensory needs.

Not all learning differences are so obvious. Most of your students probably haven't been diagnosed as having exceptional learning needs. That does not mean, however, that they do not have their own personal strengths for learning. Some people learn best visually and others through hearing. Still others learn best by touching and doing. Most people learn best if all three types of learning are involved.

Children also have various personality traits that affect their learning. Some children are quiet and introspective. Some are more outgoing and want to immediately use their learning in everyday life. Others question everything. Each student brings his or her own unique experiences (or lack of experiences) to bear on what is being discussed.

Teaching Should Differ Too

Your teaching will be much more exciting when you discover the individual strengths of your students and then teach to those strengths. You'll see those light bulbs really light up instead of just burn dimly. Watch who really seems to catch on to the story when you use pictures or who perks up the most when you do a role play of the story. Who gets most excited about a project that takes the love of Jesus outside the classroom? Do you have an artist, an author, or a musician in your class?

Even though you see each student for a short time, make it your goal to really focus on him or her during that time. Listen to what he or she says, and watch reactions to what you are doing or saying. If you have a large number of students, choose just a few to study each week. The next week, identify the strengths of several different students. Do more than teach the lesson. Teach to the strengths of your students. The whole purpose of teaching is that children learn. It's your turn to be a student again, a student of your students.

THINK ABOUT

- What are some strengths of your students that you already know?
- How can you go about identifying the strengths of all your students?
- I can teach to the strengths of my students by . . .

By this we know love, that He laid down His life for us, and we ought to lay down our lives for the brothers. But if anyone has the world's goods and sees his brother in need, yet closes his heart against him, how does God's love abide in him? Little children, let us not love in word or talk but in deed and in truth.
1 John 3:16–18

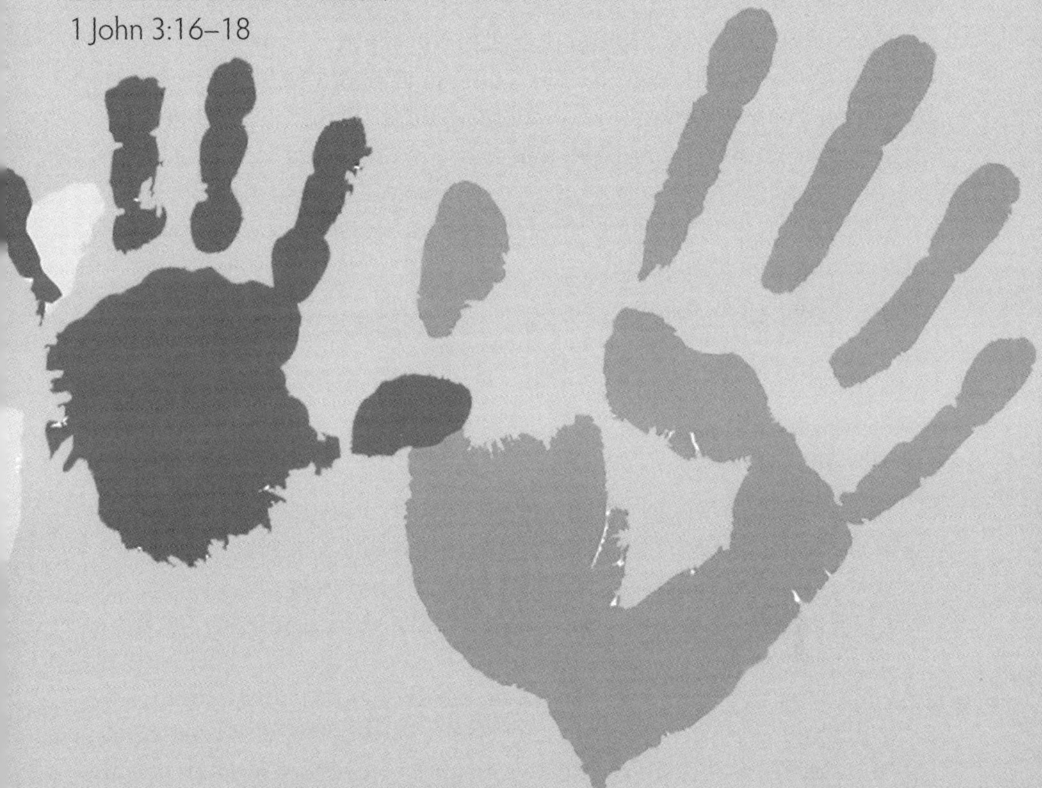

Section 4
Tools of the Trade

OPENING THOUGHT

Think about how you use the teacher guide in your planning.

The Final Edition

Lisa Krenz

Review

It will come as no surprise to you that each child God puts in your classroom is unique. Because of this, each class is unique. It would be impossible for any teacher guide to perfectly serve all the groups of children that all the teachers teach. It stands to reason that as you prepare your lesson each week, you will prepare a "final edition" that looks a bit different than the printed teacher guide and is adapted to meet the unique qualities of your group of children. You are like an expert tailor, altering the lesson to fit just right.

Two Critical Concerns

Two concerns affect how you plan your lesson. The first is *concern for your students* themselves. Plan with their unique abilities in mind, adjusting the lesson according to age, attention span, and ability to deal with abstract concepts.

It is not unusual to have a two-year age span in a single Sunday School classroom. This kind of grouping will make a difference in the activities that your students will be able to handle successfully, whether you have a class of two- to four-year-olds or a class of nine- to eleven-year-olds. Make curriculum choices based on the age span. Choose activities that are multisensory and hands-on. These activities give students opportunities to participate at their own level. Pair visual input with a chance for auditory input. If you are telling a story, also show a picture or visual aid of some kind. Add a tactile component, giving students something to touch or an action to do. Choose gross-motor activities. They help prepare the brain to do cognitive work. Teaching this way, you will reach more learners and do less adapting because each student will be involved, not just those who can confidently read and write.

The second concern you will need to address when you plan is *concern for your setting*—classroom size, number of students, teaching time, and available help. I have taught in a room that was designed to be a cry room; it did not have space for me to set up three—or even two!—different learning stations. I was also limited by time, having only thirty minutes once the children arrived from the opening session. These practical boundaries meant I needed to choose wisely from the many good activities suggested in the teacher guide. It just wasn't possible to do everything.

Addressing practical concerns contributes to good teaching. Even with a small space, you can have the students move, show pictures, do small projects, play games, and act out stories. You may just have to do things on a smaller scale. Don't give in to the temptation to be controlled by physical matters. Adapt the best activities to fit your space and time.

Adapting the Guide

Remember that the teacher guide is just that, a guide. It is flexible not fixed. You are in control of the activities you choose. Pick those that best reach your students and match their learning styles. You can change the order of things if that works best for your situation, but try to keep the new order the same every week. Routine is important for all students—especially younger ones and those with special learning needs.

Plan ahead. No adapting and fitting of your lesson to your students can happen if you don't make a plan. You will do your students a disservice if the first time you pick up your teacher guide is when the students walk into your classroom. You will not meet the needs of your students. *Planning an effective lesson doesn't take hours. Spend a short time each day during the week;* you and your students will both benefit.

The Planning Process

Sunday

Take a moment, right after class or later in the day, to briefly reflect on how the lesson went, noting activities that went well and those you might have done differently. Did the students learn and grow as you expected?

Follow your summary with a look ahead. Scan the lesson title, text, and objectives for next week. Let these components "simmer" in the back of your mind throughout the week. Pray.

Monday

Use the Bible text for your next lesson in your own personal devotion. If you use instructional material from CPH, start with the sections in your teacher guide dedicated to preparing the lesson and growing in the Word. Keep those pages with your regular devotional materials. Read the appointed Scripture passage along with these sections. This gives you the whole week to reflect on the Scripture. This is also a good time to take note of whether this section is particularly abstract for students (such as the story of Pentecost) or more concrete (such as David and Goliath). Pray.

Tuesday

Skim the teacher guide and supplementary materials for activity choices. Write down any things you may need to pick up at the store or hunt for in your cabinets to make the lesson more active and interesting. It's an awful feeling to open your teacher guide for the first time on Saturday night, only to realize that you don't have the items needed for an exciting object lesson, craft, or snack. Pray.

Wednesday

Go through the teacher guide to choose activities—those that work well for your students' unique abilities and your classroom situation. Be especially aware of students with special needs in the areas of reading, writing, vision, hearing, fine-motor skills, or attention. Put yourself in the student's place. Think: How would I feel about doing this activity if I couldn't read well?

write well? understand complex language? Whenever possible, choose multisensory activities that meet the needs of all learners—visual, auditory, and tactile/kinesthetic. Pray.

Thursday

Collect materials and practice telling the Bible narrative. Pray.

Friday or Saturday

Run through your lesson one more time. If you haven't already done so at the beginning of the quarter, separate lesson leaflets and craft pages. Punch out and prepare craft projects. If possible, set up your Sunday School room and activities. This way you won't have to rush around Sunday morning as the children are arriving. Pray.

Sunday

Pray. Relax and enjoy sharing the Good News of Jesus and His love for you and your students!

THINK ABOUT

- Planning throughout the week could help me because . . .
- How can you plan your lesson with your students' unique abilities in mind?
- How can you make the best use of your classroom setting?

OPENING THOUGHT

What strategies do you use to adapt your curriculum to meet student needs?

Curriculum Helps

Loren Sheppard

Review

Have you ever begun your lesson preparation and felt overwhelmed by the material that you needed to present? Imagine how a child with exceptional learning needs must feel on the receiving end, trying to comprehend all of the material. Your students benefit when you break your lesson down into small, manageable chunks of material. Here are some suggestions to ensure that *all* children will hear that Jesus loves them too and that, through faith in Jesus as their personal Savior, they have eternal life.

1. **Decide** which concept is the most important in the lesson, and use various materials (picture books, puzzles, word searches, drama, craft projects) to present the concept. Some lessons cover several different concepts. A child with special learning needs may only be able to comprehend one or two concepts in a class period lasting forty-five to sixty minutes. Some concepts may need to be spread out over two or three class periods. For example, if you were studying creation, with some children or classes, it might be better to discuss one day of creation per lesson. With this approach you might spend time reading about creation out of the Bible and picture books, drawing what was created, singing, and discussing the importance of that part of creation in your life. For other students or settings, it is just as helpful to cover creation all at once.
2. **Review** each week. Take five minutes to review last week's concept or story. Use timelines with pictures as well as numbers and words on the wall to show the chronological order of the Bible stories.
3. **Bulletin Boards** can be great teaching tools. When you study concepts such as the fruit of the Spirit, make an add-on bulletin board. Each week put up a different fruit to discuss from the lesson. This idea can be done with other topics as well, such as the armor of God. Then leave up the bulletin board for review and as a reminder.

4. **Posters** with the Ten Commandments or books of the Bible are a good means of review. Draw a big arrow on a piece of paper and use it to point to the commandment or book of the Bible that you are studying.
5. **Scripture interprets Scripture.** When discussing the life of Christ, pick one event and read about it in the Gospels. Then explore to see what Old Testament prophet predicted it, or read about it in other parts of the New Testament.
6. **Resources** are available. If you are having a difficult time with a lesson, take the time to consult with other teachers or the superintendent. Also, Lutheran Special Education Ministries has resources for churches, families, and schools on their Web site, www.luthsped.org.

THINK ABOUT

- The suggestions that would help my students most are . . .
- What lessons do you teach that might benefit from being spread out over several weeks?
- How can you use visual aids like timelines, bulletin boards, and posters to enhance your classroom?

OPENING THOUGHT

Why is it important not to rush learning?

God's Little Gift

Loren Sheppard

Review

Do some of your students take longer than others to understand the information presented in Sunday School each week? Children with special learning needs often take more time to internalize material. Their learning just can't be rushed. You can provide a successful learning experience for every child. Here are some suggestions:

Use Good Materials

Find an excellent curriculum that helps you teach all your students. Look for a variety of learning styles in lesson activities, options for Bible study and review, and helpful hints about teaching every child. Use a variety of presentation styles and materials—storytelling, drama, posters, music, object lessons—whatever will capture every child's attention for teaching.

Don't settle for material that fails to share the Good News about Jesus' love in every lesson, consistently and fully, every week. You have many choices for material; don't settle for anything but the best.

Repeat and Review

All children, but especially those with exceptional learning needs, benefit from hearing things more than once. Present the Bible narrative more than once using different methods. Review with questions or related activities until each child has grasped the basic message. Repeat the main point of the lesson frequently, using the same simple sentence. Take time at the end of the lesson and at the beginning of next week's class to review.

Keep It Simple

Look over the material for each quarter or the whole year, and decide what main things can be emphasized in a lesson or series of lessons. Keep these main goals in mind as you prepare and as you teach. Remember to keep the goal small enough to accomplish during the year. Children with special learning needs benefit by learning small chunks of information and building on those chunks of information each year.

Know Their Strengths

Capitalize on children's learning strengths, and determine their gifts. God has blessed each one of us with gifts to further His kingdom. Teach in ways that make the best use of the abilities of all your children, including those with special needs. Find ways that each child can put his or her gifts to use in living out a personal faith in Jesus—greeting people with a big smile as they come in to church, drawing pictures to promote a church activity or Bible truth, or participating in activities such as picking up litter or improving the community.

Each child is a blessing from God. Jesus Himself saw the value of these children and commended them as valuable in His kingdom. In our classrooms we can do the same.

THINK ABOUT

- Does the curriculum you use give you opportunities to share the Gospel consistently with every student?
- How could reviewing the main point of the lesson frequently help all of your students learn?
- I can capitalize on my students' learning strengths by . . .

OPENING THOUGHT

How do you deal with disruptive behavior in your classroom?

Teaching Tools

Loren Sheppard

Review

When you walk into your classroom, are all of your students ready and eager to hear about God's Word? Or do you have some students waiting to begin, but others distracted or disruptive? We are likely to see children of all levels of readiness and ability in our Sunday School classes. Some may have diagnosed learning disabilities. Unfortunately, volunteer teachers are not always informed of children's special learning or behavioral needs. Here are helpful tools to get you past the behavioral problems and on with the lesson.

Prayer. Before your students arrive, thank God for the opportunity to share His Word, and ask God to grant you patience and wisdom in dealing with His children. Then begin and end your lesson with prayer. Don't forget to have the children pray for others!

Structure. Try to keep the same schedule of activities each week. It may be necessary to have assigned seating so that students can be in a seat where they are not distracted.

Discipline. Find out what the discipline rules are for your Sunday School or determine them with your class. Post the rules and review them as needed. Remember that each child is important—don't focus on the misbehavior of one student. Seek help as needed from the superintendent and don't be reluctant to involve parents in solving discipline problems.

Role Model. Find another adult who is willing to team teach. When one of you teaches, the other can sit with the students who have the most difficulties completing a lesson or paying attention. It is also great to have another adult to brainstorm with about a lesson!

Variety. Teaching your lesson in three different ways can help reinforce the lesson for children with all learning needs. Use techniques tailored to a variety of learning styles, such as short videos on the Bible story, role-playing with props, choral reading, and Bible songs. Bring in objects that go with the lesson so children can see, touch, and even smell what the lesson is discussing. For example, when teaching the Lord's Supper, bring traditional unleavened bread, or bring burlap and wild honey when talking about John the Baptist. Art projects about the lesson are a fantastic way for children to express and share what they have learned with their family.

Education. Take advantage of the workshops offered in your area for Sunday and weekday schoolteachers. These can provide you with support as well as some wonderful ideas.

As you work with God's children, continue to seek His help and the help of the resources in your area.

THINK ABOUT

- My most important teaching tools are . . .
- How do I use structure and discipline in the classroom?
- How can I add variety to my lesson next week?

OPENING THOUGHT

Do you have a student who might need extra praise?

Ways to Praise

Karen Wittmayer

Review

Picture your Sunday School class. Chances are there's one student who is struggling. Perhaps it results from difficulty with reading, inability to sit still, or a tendency to make jokes that disrupt your finely tuned lesson plan for the day. Put your feet in the shoes of that child. Things may not go well in school. Sunday School may offer similar challenges. Kind words may be a rare experience.

Praise has the ability to build a child up—to build a relationship with the child and to encourage positive behavior. Here are thoughts about how this can happen.

Catch Good Behavior

It is easy to focus on negative behaviors; we often must intentionally look for good behaviors. Praise will encourage more good behavior. Use statements like "Thanks for sitting down quietly today" or "I like how you listened while others were reading."

Be Specific with Praise

Don't just say "Great" or "Good job." Look for specific actions that define good behavior and comment on them. Defining good behavior helps children understand what good behavior is and what you as a teacher expect.

Be Sincere

If you praise too often or for weak effort, praise loses its effectiveness. Children won't believe you mean it. Children are very perceptive in this.

Praise Effort, Not End Results

If a child struggles but completes an oral reading, it is more effective to say "Wow! That was tough and you kept at it" than "Great job." You both know that the reading was not really great. Let the child know that hard work pays off.

Redirect Problem Behavior

Praise positive behavior; ignore inappropriate behavior unless it is truly disruptive. If a child is trying to distract others, praise the appropriate behaviors being displayed by the others in class. This reinforces the appropriate behaviors of others, makes clear to all students the behavior that is expected, and often quickly causes a change in behavior of the child not receiving the praise. Once that child has changed his behavior, be sure to specifically praise the new, more appropriate behavior.

Paul writes in 1 Thessalonians 5:11, "Encourage one another and build one another up." Building up God's precious children through praise and encouragement can be a daunting task, especially when one has a challenging student—but what student needs it more? Remember that it is through your words and actions that children see the loving face of Christ. As we are encouraged by Christ, we can share that encouragement with all of God's children. What a privilege it is to serve our Master!

THINK ABOUT

- I can redirect problem behavior by . . .
- Why is it important to praise good behavior, not just punish bad behavior?
- What difference does specific praise make for a child?

OPENING THOUGHT

When do you interact with the parents of your students?

Parents

Lisa Krenz

Review

Parenting is a challenging endeavor—we all know this. Being the parent of a child with special needs has its own set of stressors and worries of which we may be unaware. Most of the time a Sunday School teacher doesn't have a great deal of contact with the parents of their students beyond the drop-off and pick-up times. As children get older, and more able to make their way from classroom to car, we see less and less of parents.

You may not always be aware that a student has a special need. Some special needs like physical disabilities, vision impairments, and autism are often obvious; but other special needs like learning disabilities, ADHD, and emotional disorders are not so easily noticed by nonprofessionals. In some situations, parents have struggled with school personnel to gain the services they need, so they may be fearful that you may reject their child and hesitate to share school information. In some situations, it's a struggle for parents to get their child to church on a Sunday morning. If you notice a child in church that you know has a special need, make it a point to invite him or her to Sunday School. Parents may not realize their child is welcome.

Learning to Welcome

Regardless of the child's special need, the best first comment a teacher could make to a parent is always an enthusiastic, "I'm so happy to have your child (use the child's name) in my class." Begin the conversation with something positive that you've noticed about their child. Ask the parents to tell you more about what their child likes and excels at. Find a way to connect to each child's gift. Continue by reassuring the parent that the child is welcome and you will do whatever it takes to make his/her time in your class meaningful.

If the parent shares that their child receives special education services at school, ask them if they think the child's IEP (Individual Education Plan) has any information that may be helpful in the Sunday School setting such as behavior management plans and accommodations and modifications made to curriculum. Many times it is negative behaviors that impede successful integration into Sunday School, not academic ability. Ask parents what strategies work best for teachers at school or for them at home. An extra helper in class can go a long way to mitigate negative behaviors for all students. Resist the temptation to ask the parent to act as this aide. The parent needs the opportunity to participate in their own Bible studies and the child needs the opportunity to interact with their same-aged peers.

You may only have a couple of minutes here and there, but make it a point to connect with parents either after church, after Sunday School, or by phone. Start with a smile and end with a smile. Pray for all your students and their families. The Lord will show you the way.

THINK ABOUT

- I can support families of children with special needs by . . .
- What joys and struggles might parents of a child with special needs encounter?
- What things can I pray for to benefit the families of all my students?

I thank You, Father, Lord of heaven and earth, that You have hidden these things from the wise and understanding and revealed them to little children; yes, Father, for such was Your gracious will.
Matthew 11:25–26

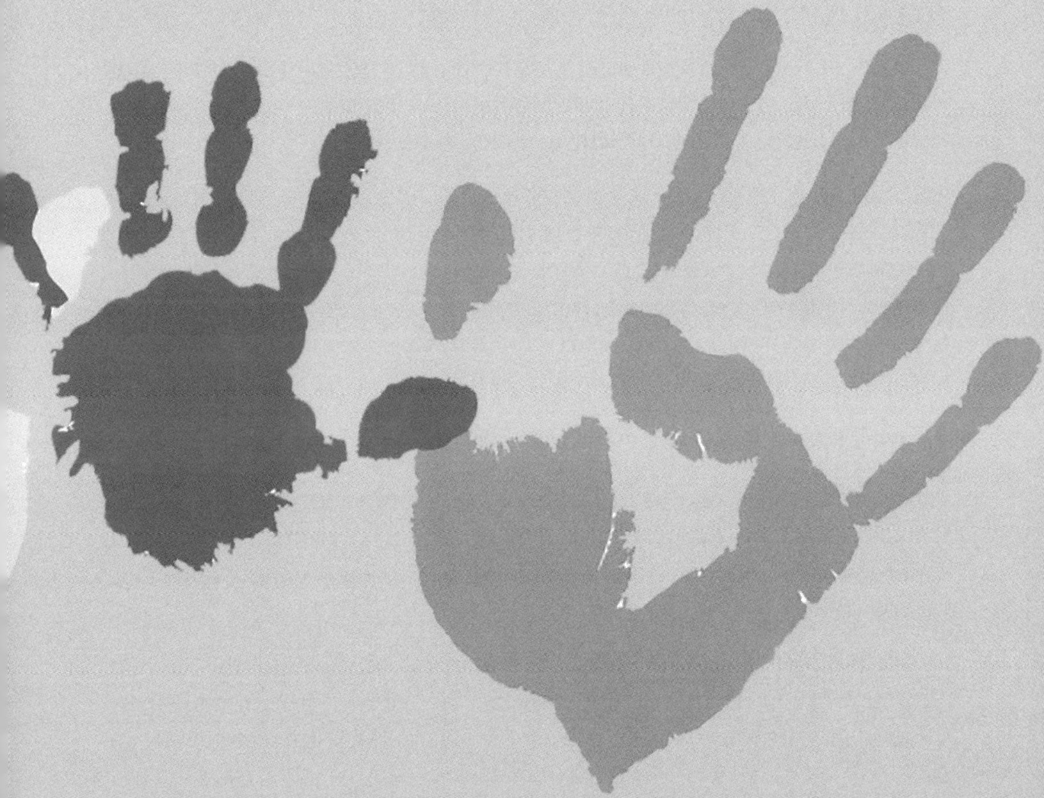

Section 5

Putting Children First

OPENING THOUGHT

How do you like to be identified?

A Student Who Is Blind

Dave Andrus

Review

Teachers of Sunday School meet kids from many different kinds of families. Each is unique and special. Jesus loves them all. But some teachers might ask, "How do I interact and work with a student who is blind?"

The most important thing to remember is the blindness does not make the child. He or she is a person, just like the others in your class. He or she may learn or read differently but don't let this dictate their identity. Each person has particular weaknesses and strengths. Just as with other students, take the time to get to know a student who is blind as a person and appreciate the strengths he or she has. Focus on him or her as a person first.

People First Language

Because a disability may be conspicuous, we too often focus on it first rather than on the person. People First Language helps us to reorient our thinking about and speaking to persons with disabilities, giving them the same focus we hope others will give to us.

People First Language uses phrases that affirm the person, not the disability. This method also uses words and phrases that make the person more than the disability. Its usage describes what the person HAS, not who the person IS.

Preferred	Not Preferred
A man who is blind	A blind man
People who are blind	The blind
A man who is deaf	A deaf mute
People who are deaf	The deaf
A man who cannot walk	A cripple
A person who is not mobile	An invalid
A man who has learning disabilities	A dumb or stupid man
A man who has developmental disabilities	A mentally retarded man
A man with bipolar disorder	A bipolar
A man who has schizophrenia	A schizophrenic
A man who is speechless	A dumb man

People who have physical disabilities, like blindness, already deal with a lot of earthly brokenness and pain. We do not want to needlessly add to their hardships. They often feel the application of the Law heavily in their lives through their physical condition. It is therefore important that other Christians—people of the Gospel—share, show, and teach the Gospel prominently with people so affected. Jesus Himself experienced physically brokenness. He accepts people who have disabilities. A person who has a physical disability can identify with and find his or her identity in the Wounded Physician (1 Peter 2:24).

SALE (Stop. Ask. Listen. Evaluate.)

The acronym SALE serves as a helpful tool to use when dealing with a child or adult with noticeable disabilities.

Stop: Do not immediately do what your instincts suggest. We all want to help, but what is the correct help or service? This must be determined.

Ask: The best and easiest way to determine what should be done, if anything, is to ask: "Is there anything I can do to assist you?"

Listen: It is one thing to ask a person what he or she wants or needs but it is still another, and far more important, thing to hear what he or she said. It is insulting to ask a person but then to do what we think he or she needs. If their answer is unclear or vague, you may want to ask clarifying questions, "Are you saying that you would like to . . . ? Do you want me to help you or shall I stand back?"

Evaluate: Sometimes when asked, a person who is blind will indicate that he or she needs no help. They know where they are going or how to do a task. It is right and proper to observe as they then go about their way. If you observe that he or she has gone astray or is bewildered, again SALE:

Stop: Do not rush in as though to rescue him or her.

Ask: "You seem to be in a corner. Do you need help?"

Listen: The answer they give may surprise you. They may not be lost or they may want to learn better their surroundings or they may say yes, they want assistance.

Evaluate: When a person who is blind is truly lost and bewildered, a friendly, helpful voice is welcome.

Resources

Braille and large-print Bibles, devotionals, and other Christian resources are available at no cost from Lutheran Braille Workers: www.lbwinc.org or by calling 800-925-6092.

THINK ABOUT

- I can incorporate People First Language into my everyday life by . . .
- If you have a student who is blind in your class, how can you best accommodate for his or her needs?
- Describe a situation in which SALE would be helpful.

OPENING THOUGHT

When I don't know the answer to a question, I . . .

Help! I Don't Know What That Means

Lisa Krenz

Review

The Sunday School hour is over, and you're packing up your things to go home. A woman with an unfamiliar face approaches you apprehensively. "Hi, my name is Mandy, and my son is old enough to be in your class."

"Terrific!" you reply enthusiastically. "What's his name?"

"His name is Tommy." She looks relieved but still a little unsure. "Well, I just wanted you to know. Tommy has an IEP at school. He has LD and ADHD and has a little trouble sometimes. Do you think he can still come to Sunday School?"

Your instinct is to welcome every new student, but you may also have a moment of panic. What is an IEP? What do LD and ADHD mean? What are you getting into?

This situation is played out in Sunday Schools all across the country. The specific special needs may be different, but the picture is the same. Children with special learning needs often bring with them an alphabet soup of terms that might confuse or intimidate you. When a parent or a professional teacher has been dealing with these terms for a long time, it's easy to forget that not everyone knows what an IEP (individualized education plan) is or what LD (learning disability) and ADHD (attention deficit hyperactivity disorder) mean. In different situations someone might refer to PDD (pervasive developmental disorder) or ID (intellectual disability) or CP (cerebral palsy) or a whole dictionary full of other foreign sounding acronyms and words.

Fear of the unknown is a typical reaction. The good news is that the unknown can easily be changed to known. Information is just a click or a call away. Information is your armor against fear. Start with the parents. Don't be embarrassed to say, "I'm sorry, I'm not familiar with that term, but I think it would help me be a better teacher if I knew more." Remember, this information was new to that parent once also. They are your first resource.

The Internet is a vast resource. Many specific areas of special needs have Web sites created by professional organizations to share information about their area of concern. Examples of this are www.ldonline.com, www.autismspeaks.org, and www.cerebralpalsy.org. Agencies like Bethesda Lutheran Communities also have Web sites (www.bethesdalutherancommunities.org) to share information more specific to religious instruction. These examples are just the tip of a very large iceberg.

Check your congregation for people resources. Special education teachers and public school educators may not want to teach Sunday School after teaching all week, but they will be more than happy to share information and teaching ideas. Invite them to be a sounding board for your questions and thoughts about the best way to run your classroom. Certainly, the Holy Spirit will guide you as you seek to share the Gospel. Fear not, for you are not alone.

THINK ABOUT

- What apprehensions might parents have when they bring their child to Sunday School?
- How can you ease parents' apprehensions?
- How will getting information make you a better teacher?

OPENING THOUGHT

How would you include a student with Down syndrome in your Sunday School classroom?

How Many Sleeps till Sunday?

Karen Wittmayer

Review

One Sunday morning, a family got up and got ready for church. Their son, Adam, was especially excited because he got to go to Sunday School. Adam knew he would learn about Jesus. In fact, throughout the week, he had been asking his mom and dad how many more sleeps until he could go back to Sunday School and learn more about Jesus.

Adam loves Sunday School and is learning to know and trust in Jesus. This tells us several things about the Sunday School he attends. It is Christ-centered and accepting. It is also inclusive, because this young man, who dearly loves his Savior and his Sunday School, has Down syndrome.

A few simple suggestions will help a Sunday School teacher reach and teach a child with Down syndrome.

Include Every Child

Don't hesitate to include a child with Down syndrome in a class with same-aged peers. With appropriate adjustments in the teacher's expectations and a small amount of extra preparation, a child with Down syndrome feels included.

Emphasize Concrete Teaching

Intellectually, children with Down syndrome face many challenges, but they are able to learn and participate in class. They can remember the basic points of a story. Higher level thinking may be more difficult, so when asking questions in class, always ask them concrete questions about facts from the story.

Monitor Attention Spans

Short attention spans are also common among students with Down syndrome. To help them, break lessons or activities into short chunks. Use visuals and involve other senses that support learning. To maintain a child's attention, use that child's name or stand close to him or her.

Employ strategies that work to minimize distractions, such as keeping the student away from the window, reducing noise, and maintaining an orderly classroom where students know your expectations, routines, and rules.

Encourage Appropriate Behavior

Typically, children with Down syndrome do not display behavior problems. When needed, guide them with positive comments to reinforce appropriate behavior. A special helper can shadow them, providing assistance and reminding them of appropriate classroom behaviors. Good teaching involves routines that have positive effects on the behavior of all children.

Adam went to Sunday School that morning and was greeted with hugs by his teacher and the helper. His parents were able to go to their Bible class knowing that their son was loved, accepted, and safe. With prayer and preparation, you can make your Sunday School classroom a place where all of God's children learn of His love. Perhaps they all will be asking their parents, "How many sleeps till I get to go to Sunday School?"

THINK ABOUT

- I can make my teaching more concrete by . . .
- How do I make students aware of classroom expectations?
- How could these suggestions help every child in my classroom?

OPENING THOUGHT

What do you know about people who have autism?

When Autism Meets Sunday School

Lisa Krenz

Review

Autism knows no boundaries of race, creed, or socioeconomic situation. According to the Autism Society, as many as 1.5 million Americans today are believed to have some form of autism. Chances are good that, at some point, you will have a student with autism in your class. What will you do?

Be Informed

First, gather information. Fear of the unknown is your worst enemy. The more you know about autism and about your individual student's strengths and weaknesses, the better equipped you will be to handle things in your classroom. The Autism Society (www.autism-society.org) is a good place to start gathering basic information. Parents or caregivers will also know many resources and strategies for behavior management and learning.

Talk with the parents. Assure them that their child is welcome in your class and that surely God will bless all of you through their child. Many emotions are involved with being the parent of a child with autism. They range from fear to frustration, from great elation over new accomplishments to great sorrow over dreams that may never come true.

Typical characteristics of children who are diagnosed with autism include communication delays; limited social skills and interaction with others; engaging in repetitive behavior such as hand flapping, object spinning, and insistence on sameness; and sensory processing issues—either overly attuned to stimulus or under stimulated. Some children with autism appear to be "in their own world" and make very little eye contact, but the behaviors associated with autism occur on a very broad continuum. Each child with this diagnosis will still have his or her own personality and unique gifts, abilities, and particular areas of struggle.

Enlist Help

One of the most effective ways for a child with autism to be included in Sunday School is for that child to have an aide or helper who shadows the student, assisting the student in staying on task, relieving stress when needed, and adapting activities as appropriate. This would provide the student with needed support as well as freeing up the teacher to teach the lessons and manage the rest of the class. This aide will free up the child's parent or caregiver to attend Bible class and gives the student someone else to connect with at church.

Since many children with autism seem to be "in their own world," you may or may not be sure how much of your message is getting through. Be assured that the Holy Spirit is working in this child. You may not be the one to reap the harvest, but keep planting God's Word with full confidence that it will not return empty.

THINK ABOUT

- I can welcome a student with autism into my classroom by . . .
- How could a teacher aide help the student? the teacher? the parents?
- In what ways might God bless you and your class through a student with autism?

OPENING THOUGHT

Do you keep a cluttered or an open classroom?

Is Your Room Ready?

Lisa Krenz

Review

One of the joys of teaching is getting to know each unique individual that comes into your classroom. You quickly discover various strengths, interests, and even weaknesses that your students possess. Sometimes you may have knowledge of a student's particular limitation prior to their arrival, as in the case of children with physical or sensory disabilities. While such situations are rare compared to the incidence of students with hidden disabilities, such as learning disabilities or attention deficit disorder, being prepared for such a student will go a long way toward getting to know the child once he or she arrives in your class.

For instance, there are many ways you can adapt your classroom and your teaching to include a student who is visually impaired. A student with a visual impairment may be either blind (total loss of sight) or partially sighted (some limited vision). Knowing the extent of your student's vision loss will guide you in how you adapt printed materials and classroom activities.

- Remove obstacles and clutter from the room.
- To orient the student to the room, take a tour of the room when the student arrives each Sunday.
- When speaking about where things are located, use clock-face positioning, placing yourself at "12 o'clock."
- Be consistent in where you place things in the room so that the student can find things as independently as possible.
- Have other students take turns serving as the student's assistant.
- Provide students with materials in large print or braille. (Check with the Lutheran Library for the Blind.) The copy machine is also a good way to make large-print materials.
- Bring in teaching items that students can touch and manipulate.

- Make papers more tactile by adding glitter glue or gluing on yarn around the borders of pictures.
- Let students color over something with textures (such as corrugated cardboard or sandpaper) to produce shapes or pictures.
- Check with parents for any specific strategies that the child uses at home or in school.

The New Testament has various accounts of Jesus healing people who were blind. As with many miraculous healing accounts, such events do not usually take place in the same ways today. When these stories come up, assure students that Jesus' love for them is real for us now and that all of us will receive ultimate healing in heaven one day. Remind all students that none of us can see Jesus with our eyes. It is only by faith, given us by the Holy Spirit through Word and Sacraments, that any of us can see our Savior, Jesus.

THINK ABOUT

- I can welcome a student who is blind by . . .
- How can you incorporate tactile objects into your next lesson?
- Which of these suggestions could help all of your students?

Communication Problems

Lisa Krenz

OPENING THOUGHT

Think of a time when you were at a loss for words.

Review

Have you ever been in a group of people speaking a different language and were therefore unable to participate? Have you experienced the frustration of not being able to remember the words you need to communicate your thoughts? It is easy to feel inadequate in such situations. We take the ability to communicate for granted and often evaluate others based on how well they express themselves. There may be children in your Sunday School, however, who cannot communicate through the use of speech. A physical disability, like cerebral palsy, might be impairing the connection between brain messages and muscles needed to produce speech. A neurological impairment like autism might be hindering the communication process in other ways. These students face some unique difficulties, but one thing is certain. The ability to produce speech does not need to be a prerequisite for attending Sunday School. Here are some tips for making their time in your class fruitful.

It's Not a Hearing Problem

First, assume that the child who cannot speak *can* still hear and understand you. No need to speak loud or use baby talk.

Remember that we can't really know the cognitive functioning of a person who cannot communicate. It's better to overestimate cognitive skills rather than underestimate. Assume that the child is taking in and storing all that you are teaching them and be confident that the Holy Spirit is working through the Word in the life of that child.

Find another communication method. Picture or word cards, electronic systems provided by parents, and sign language are all options. Take time to learn how to use any communication system that the family is using.

Understand that behavior issues may stem from frustration at the inability to communicate. Don't punish a child because you can't understand his wants and needs.

Include the child in activities and a class with peers of the same age. Encourage friendships between this student and others. Point out things they have in common. Pair the student with a sensitive classmate. Get out of the way and let them develop their own way to be friends. Kids are often much better at this when we aren't hovering.

Enlist Help

It might be a good idea to have an extra aide in the classroom to shadow and assist a student with communication issues. Communicate with parents so they can communicate with their child. Write a note by the end of class: "Becky was Jennifer's helper today. They seemed to have a good time, lots of smiles. We talked about Jesus and the temple. You can read the story at home on the leaflet."

As with all teaching, working with students with communication disorders requires patience. In His grace, God gives us the fruit of the Spirit in our teaching; love, joy, peace, patience, kindness, goodness, faithfulness, gentleness, and self-control (Galatians 5:22–23).

THINK ABOUT

- I can welcome a student with a communication issue by . . .
- How can you provide information for the family of a student with communication issues?
- God can reach a student with communication issues because . . .

OPENING THOUGHT

How do you react when in a new and unfamiliar situation?

Learning about Learning Disabilities

Karen Wittmayer

Review

More frequently than ever, Sunday School teachers are discovering that children in their classes have diagnosed conditions that impact learning. How will you handle a class with such diverse needs? Here are clear, basic definitions and strategies for some learning differences you may encounter.

Dyslexia

Students with dyslexia typically have normal intelligence but find reading and/or writing activities to be painfully slow and laborious. They display difficulties with oral or silent reading, reading comprehension, spelling, or written language. To accommodate these children, allow them to volunteer for reading or answering questions; highlight and shorten sections to be read; teach and review small chunks of the story; frequently review key words; provide peer partners; seat such children near you; stand near while giving directions; reduce the need for written responses; allow oral answers; use hands-on activities; and provide models and examples.

ADHD

ADHD (Attention Deficit Hyperactivity Disorder) is a condition that makes it difficult to control behavior and pay attention. Children with this condition may display inattention, hyperactivity, impulsivity, or a combination of these traits. Inattentive children benefit from sitting close to the teacher, where redirection can be ongoing. All children with ADHD benefit from classroom routines and structure; consistent expectations and rules; eye contact; simple, step-by-step instruction; activities involving directed movement; and specific praise for targeted behavior.

Asperger's Syndrome

Children with Asperger's syndrome typically have normal to above average intelligence and can be very verbal, especially about topics they love; however, they demonstrate weaknesses in social skills, the inability to read social situations, and a strong reliance on patterns and routines. They may be especially sensitive to light, sound, and touch; lack common sense; and be very concrete thinkers. A Sunday School teacher can help these children by providing consistent routine; preparing the child ahead of time for changes; encouraging and modeling social interaction; and explaining and reviewing key terms, especially those that are abstract.

In addition, these general strategies are important whenever you scratch your head and wonder, "What can I do?" Talk with parents about strategies they use at home. And pray. Pray for wisdom, strength, and patience. Pray for the child and the child's family. Pray, knowing that God always hears and answers in wisdom and love.

THINK ABOUT

- I can welcome a student with dyslexia by . . .
- I can welcome a student with ADHD by . . .
- I can welcome a student with Asperger's syndrome by . . .

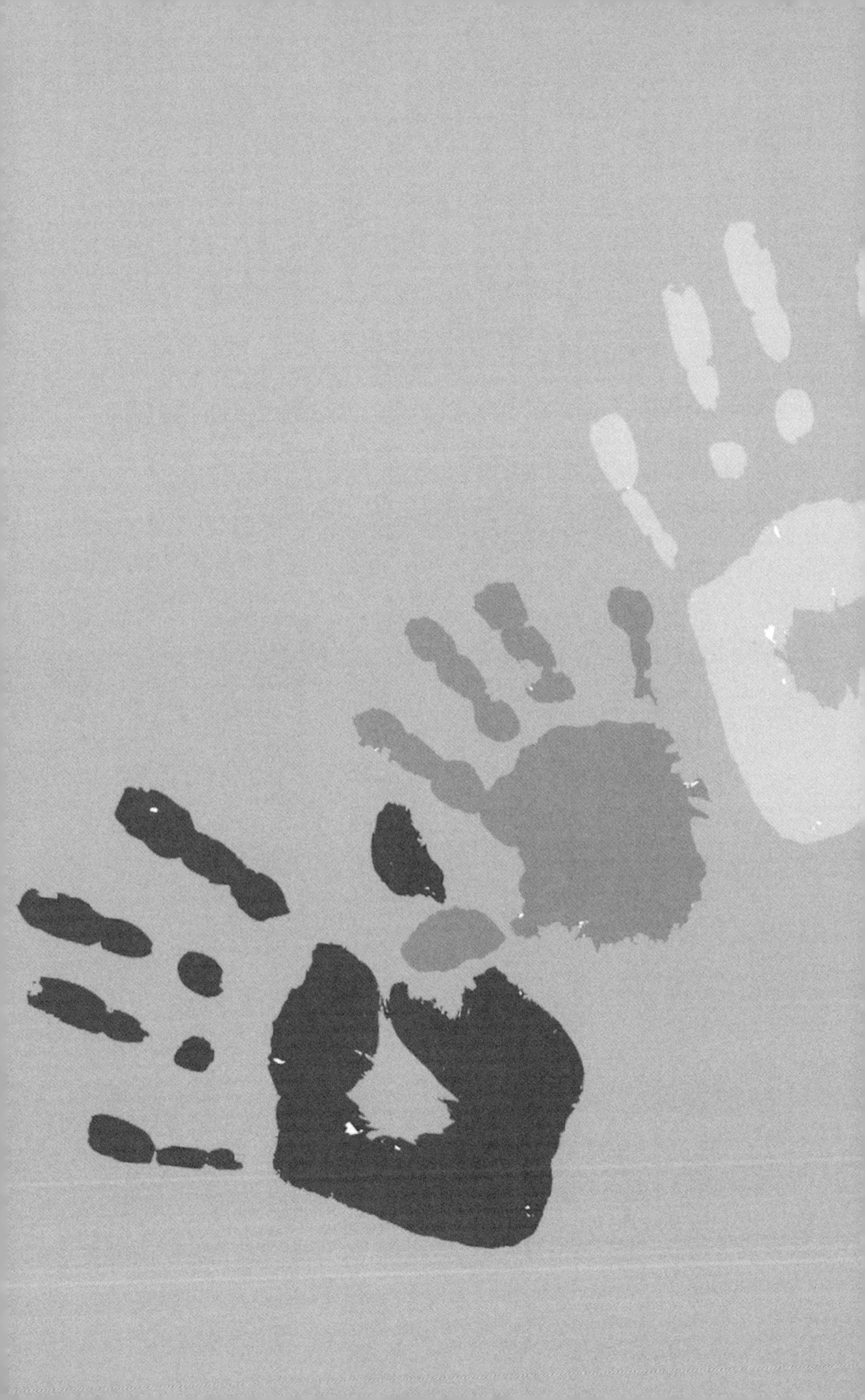

May my teaching drop as the rain, my speech distill as the dew, like gentle rain upon the tender grass, and like showers upon the herb. For I will proclaim the name of the LORD; ascribe greatness to our God!
Deuteronomy 32:2–3

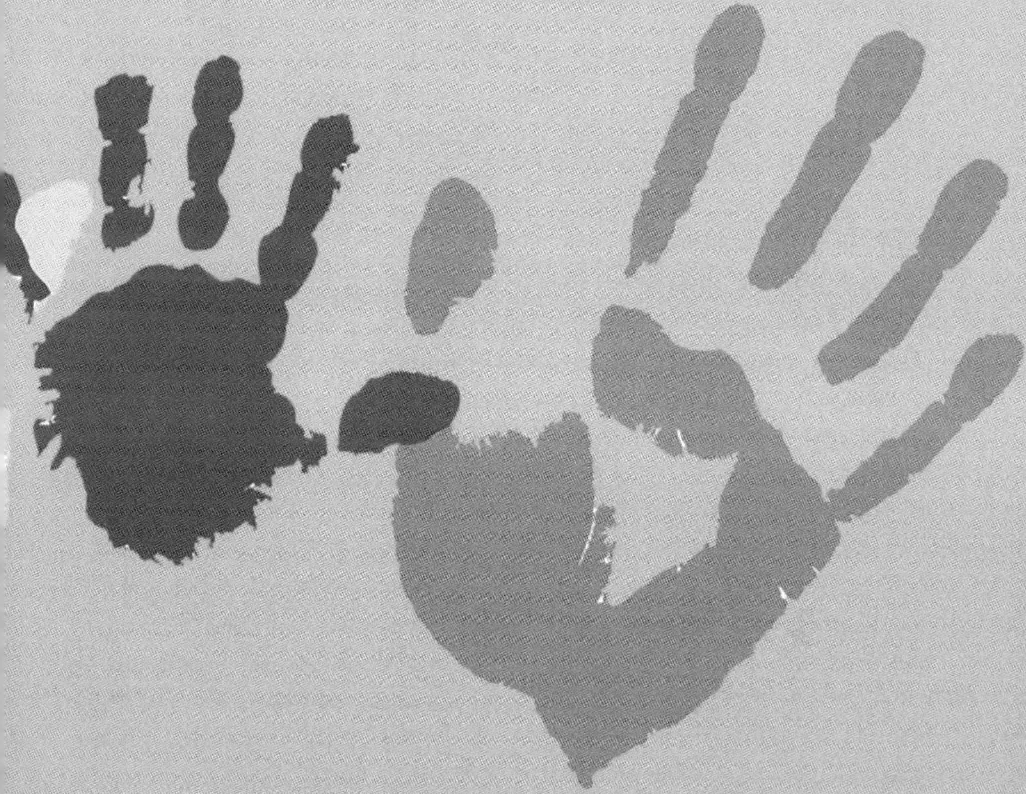

Section 6
Seeing the Invisible Need

OPENING THOUGHT

Think of a time you made an incorrect assumption based on appearance.

What You Can't See

Lisa Krenz

Review

"Don't judge a book by its cover"—we've heard this saying our whole lives. We know it's true, but we do it anyway. How often do we make assumptions about children based on what we see on the outside, when we know the best part of people is really on the inside, their hearts, their creativity, their humor?

A Learning Disability

By definition, a learning disability is something that can't be seen on the outside. Kids with learning disabilities look like every other child in the room. A learning disability is identified when a child has average to above average cognitive ability and thus would be expected to read, write, do math, or process information like other children his or her age. But for some reason we don't clearly understand that the child is not able to achieve academically at the commensurate levels with their same-aged peers even after educational interventions. Educators call this unexpected underachievement and even with interventions a student with a learning disability doesn't get caught up as quickly as we would expect. Deficits may appear in areas of reading, writing, math, spelling, memory, and information processing. Some students with learning disabilities might also struggle with attention or social skills. None of this makes them unable to learn, they just need to learn in a different way. As you can imagine, a learning disability manifests itself differently in each child, but there are some common threads—strong cognitive ability, lower academic achievement levels, lack of response to interventions.

Even if you don't know for sure that some of your students have a learning disability, just assume someone does. According to the Learning Disabilities Association of America, approximately 6 percent of school-aged children receive special education services for learning disabilities.

Seeing the Unseen

Since a learning disability can't be readily noticed like a physical disability, how will you know if one of your students in Sunday School has a learning disability? Since you don't teach Reading, English, and Math on Sunday morning, you might not notice that a student has a learning disability like a regular classroom teacher might. The good news—it's not up to you to refer a child for special education or make a diagnosis. It's just up to you to be sensitive to the learning needs of all your students. Here are some signals that might be displayed in students with learning disabilities.

Avoidance Behaviors—Acting out is often preferable for a student than looking "stupid" or "dumb" so you may see students misbehaving when it's time for the class to read aloud or do worksheets. You might also notice that the child with reading deficits conveniently has to go to the restroom just before it's his or her turn to read aloud in class. Don't just assume that a child has a behavior problem; disruptive behaviors may indicate a learning problem.

Academic Deficiencies—This child reads in a halting manner, struggles to sound out words, engages their whole body when reading, has no idea what they have just read to you. You might also note that this child's handwriting is immature, pencil grip is awkward, and papers are riddled with misspellings and erasures.

Language Processing—Some students with learning disabilities might be able to chatter all day but not really say anything, or just the opposite, talk very little for fear of saying something that exposes their learning problem. This student might struggle to find the word that he or she really wants to use, talking all around a subject but never quite "nailing it." This child might also have trouble following multistep directions. The more abstract and complex language that comes from Bible stories and catechism may be problematic unless put into concrete terms.

Social Skills Deficits—Problems reading a page sometimes translate into problems "reading" a social situation. This student might interrupt or consistently say things off topic or inappropriate. They seem not to have a "filter" on the thoughts that come out of their mouth. Sometimes this child seems socially awkward or immature.

Attention Issues—This student gets "lost" easily, they miss steps in the activity, they misunderstand the language and before long they drift off to something else that captures their interest.

I Can Learn

Remember, a child with a learning disability certainly can learn. He or she may need to learn in a different way or a different pace. When planning your lesson, think about including these teaching strategies:

- Use active learning to get everyone moving. Use music with actions. Role-play the story.
- Use multiple senses in your presentation and activities.
- Make connections to real life. Make it concrete.
- Ask for volunteers to read rather than putting anyone on the spot.
- Give writing models to copy.
- Reduce choices and manage sensory overload.

Create multiple means of presentation and participation. Don't just tell the story in one way or ask the children to respond in one way. If a child doesn't write well, what's another way to respond? If coming up with the right word to speak is difficult, can the child respond by pointing to a picture or doing an action? If reading is difficult, how can you show the story so the child can hear it and see it?

For many students, the best gift you can give is the gift of time; the time to process the incoming information, the time to generate the accurate outgoing information.

Faith is not measured by how effectively a child reads, writes, speaks, or does math. Of course when teaching a lesson in Sunday School, a teacher thrills to hear the "right answers" from the class, and those responses certainly help us to know that our students are comprehending what we are teaching, but the immediate right answer isn't the only product of our teaching. Students also learn about faith from watching you, their teacher, share the love of Christ with them in multiple and creative ways.

THINK ABOUT

- I can look for unseen disabilities in my classroom by . . .
- Which suggestions can you implement next week?
- How many of these suggestions could help more than one student?

OPENING THOUGHT

Have you ever been punished for something outside your control?

Hide and Seek

Lisa Krenz

Review

Who's in your Sunday School class? Bobby and Sally? Brittany and Dakota? Destinee and Demondre? If you took a class picture, you might see pigtails and gap-toothed smiles, church dresses and tights, or neatly buttoned collars. A class roster or group photo can't begin to tell the story of who is in your class. You won't really be able to answer that question even after the first lesson. It takes time to go beyond the obvious, beyond the first impressions and assumptions, before we can truly know a child.

What we do know about our students is that God created each and every one of them, unique and blessed with their own special gifts. Jesus loves each one so much that He was willing to die on a cross so they, too, might have eternal life with Him in heaven. A child's special needs are often hidden behind sweet faces and well-dressed facades. Not all children with special needs come with wheelchairs, hearing aids, talking devices, or the obvious indicators of differences. Because there is no physical manifestation, one of the most challenging aspects of some special needs is that unknowing adults can be judgmental and harsh regarding behaviors and skills that do not measure up to expectations. The list of special needs that are hidden is long and varied. Learning disabilities, attention deficit disorders, emotional disorders, autism spectrum disorder, Asperger's, and giftedness all fall in this realm. Sometimes, parents will share this type of information with Sunday School teachers; other times, they won't.

Root Cause

Although it's easy to jump to the conclusion that misbehavior is the result of a naughty child, negative behaviors commonly hide more complex issues. Reading deficits, sensory overload, boredom, and an inability to regulate actions and emotions can all lead to behaviors not well suited to the standard Sunday School classroom. The good news is that it's not up to you to make a diagnosis or to be an expert. It's your job to share the Gospel with that child and to show how much Jesus loves him or her. It's your job to seek out how each child learns best and to find interesting and engaging ways to share each week's lesson. When you notice behaviors that get in the way of learning, dig a little deeper, consider other options, do some research, and diversify your activities in new ways. Seek a new solution.

Put yourself in the child's seat. What would it be like if you couldn't read like your classmates? What if writing and spelling were laborious for you? Is the Sunday School classroom overstimulating and unpredictable? What if you read and understand at a level far above everyone else but have trouble understanding social situations? Consider what would be more engaging in relation to the above-mentioned issues. Talk to other teachers and the child's parents. Check the Internet for ideas related to specific special needs. Above all, seek to find the special someone hiding inside each and every one of your students.

THINK ABOUT

- I can help students with hidden disabilities in my classroom by . . .
- What might cause your "naughty" students to misbehave?
- What can you do to change your perspective and actions next week?

OPENING THOUGHT

Think of a time you were embarrassed because you were asked to do something you had trouble doing.

Help! Sammy Can't Read!

Karen Wittmayer

Review

Picture this familiar Sunday scene: You've just begun your Sunday School class for the morning, welcomed a new student named Sammy to your class, passed out the lesson leaflets and Bibles, and are ready to begin. You proceed to assign each child a few Bible verses to read. Soon it's your new student's turn and you discover, to your great dismay, that Sammy can barely read the verses and, in fact, reads much below the level of the rest of the students in your class. You panic and think to yourself, "What do I do now?" First, let's think about Sammy's perspective on this reading problem.

Sammy's Perspective: What This Feels Like to Him

- I just seem to get stuck when I try to read a lot of words.
- It takes me so long to read something.
- Reading is so hard; I can't think about what it means.
- The words are too hard.
- There's too many of them on a page.
- I can't read well because the print is too small.

Almost every teacher, whether volunteer or professional, has experienced having a child with underdeveloped reading skills in class. Your first thought is to just skip the child's next turn to read, but you realize this may hurt his or her feelings and make him or her feel left out. Next you decide to just go ahead and let the child read again, but as he or she struggles with each word, you see cheeks turning red with embarrassment and frustration. Let's think about some easy adaptations you can make to your lesson.

What Teachers Can Do at Sunday School

- Recognize that reading fluency issues will not be fixed at Sunday School.
- Use choral reading, assigning passages to groups of students to read orally.
- Provide the child with an index card as a guide during reading.
- Plan ahead, subtly assigning shorter reading selections to the child who struggles.
- Ask the child's parents for insights into the child's learning style.

Children with delayed oral reading skills and fluency often feel very self-conscious about their weakness and are reluctant readers. Then, as the child grows older, this self-consciousness, reluctance, and frustration increases. Chances are that this child has been diagnosed with a learning disability in reading and is receiving special help at school. However, this disability affects Sunday School too.

Pray specifically for the Sammys in your classroom. Pray that their learning difficulties won't hamper their desire to learn. Pray that you will successfully adapt the lessons. Most important, pray that through God's Word, the children will have faith in Jesus as the kind and loving Savior who has chosen them to be His very own.

THINK ABOUT

- Which of these suggestions can you implement next week to help readers who struggle?
- How can you decrease a student's self-consciousness and frustration about reading?
- I can make my classroom more welcoming to every student by . . .

OPENING THOUGHT

How could Sunday School be an overwhelming environment for some children?

Dysregulated Children

Lisa Krenz

Review

Sunday School is stressful. How can that be? My Sunday School class is fun—no memory work, lots of hands-on activities, snacks, and music. How is that stressful?

Have you seen any of these students in your classroom?

- the child in the corner with his sweatshirt pulled up over his head, refusing to participate
- the child who is glued to your side the entire class, blurting out unrelated comments throughout the lesson
- the child using bad language and picking fights
- the child standing on the table when you walk into the room
- the child with the inexplicable temper tantrums and meltdowns
- the brooding child who doesn't say a word all class
- the child who refuses to put the stickers where you direct or follow along with activities and seems not to care about reward charts

All of these are examples of children who are demonstrating signs of emotional dysregulation. They are feeling stressed and overwhelmed by their environment even when we don't realize it, sometimes even when we think we are providing a fun, therefore nonstressful, environment.

Occasionally or Often?

Most children demonstrate some of these behaviors on occasion. We've all observed a toddler who melts down or a preteen who broods. You may be asking yourself, "What's the difference between a naughty child and one who is dysregulated?" Children who have these behaviors on a consistent basis are not naughty; they are out of control. Their actions are a cry for help. They are so stressed internally that they can't control their behaviors. They are dysregulated.

Children with many different types of special needs can suffer from dysregulation. It is important to realize these disruptive students are most often dealing with issues about which you are unaware. Their anger may cover feelings of worthlessness, fear of rejection or shame, or overstimulation. We don't know the situation, and we may never know it.

Love Them

These students may not be easy to be with. Some of them may be downright exhausting. However, these challenging children need us. Positive, loving relationships will help them feel respected and valued. Our loving actions will often calm them enough to participate more normally in the class.

Jesus tells us, "Let the little children come to Me" (Matthew 19:14). He doesn't qualify His statement, saying invite only the cute, well-behaved, obedient, and cheerful children. None of our students will be perfect. Each will struggle with sin and the burden of a sinful nature, and Jesus invites them all. The Lord does not leave us without help in our task, though. Whether you feel it or not, know that the Holy Spirit is hard at work, using you to build relationships and share the Gospel with this child and his or her family. Read the next article, "So Now What Do I Do?" for more detailed strategies for helping dysregulated children.

THINK ABOUT

- I can welcome children who are emotionally dysregulated by . . .
- A child might be emotionally dysregulated because . . .
- How can you show these children the love of Jesus and His peace?

OPENING THOUGHT

Review what you know about emotional dysregulation.

So Now What Do I Do?

Lisa Krenz

Review

Since reading "Dysregulated Children," you've been mulling over the idea of children who are emotionally dysregulated and the whole concept is making sense to you. When the child is stressed, their frontal lobe shuts down and they shift away from learning mode and into survival mode. Behaviors become less rational. What is a teacher to do?

In the short term, you will do what you must to smooth the troubled water and continue with your teaching task. When a child begins to display dysregulated behavior, be a source of calmness and self-control. They cannot regulate their behavior. You can regulate yours. Visibly regulate yourself. Keep your voice soft. Take deep breaths. The child needs a calm outside world to learn regulation. Never demean a child. Stay out of power struggles. Give the child control by giving them choices. Having a second adult present who can assist or even take an upset child for a walk may be helpful.

Thinking about the long term will be the most effective strategy for dealing with the dysregulated child.

Relationships

Smaller student-teacher ratios are preferable. This gives you more opportunities for one-on-one attention and relationship building.

Find a connection. Investigate what the child is interested in and use that as a starting point. Make eye contact and smile across the narthex or in church. Send a note, quick e-mail, or text during the week just to say, "Hi, I'm praying for you."

The tough love, demanding approach won't work. Any kind of shaming is counterproductive. (Even something like a sticker chart for attendance or good behavior can be shaming when that child's chart is empty of stickers.)

Make your classroom a safe place emotionally. Remember that this child may be very bright but may have unexpected gaps in understanding or skill. Don't put the students on the spot. Let them volunteer when they are ready. They may not share answers or fill in worksheets, but they benefit from being in your class. Trust that the Holy Spirit is using you to share the Good News of Jesus.

Stability

Enter the room with a deep breath and a prayer. Don't be surprised or dismayed by dysregulation. Plan for it. You will be pleasantly surprised by how much more smoothly things will go.

Seating charts and schedules are helpful. Predictability is very important, for the child and for you. Something as simple as knowing where he or she will sit will mitigate a child's anxiety. Prepare the child for transitions and changes.

Stimulus

Look for ways to reduce distraction or chaos. You cannot control everything in your Sunday School classroom, but minimize where you can. Keep the child's workspace clear of unused items. Keep the challenging child close to you and away from pencil sharpeners, windows, toys, and other distractions. Allowing the child to chew gum, suck on a mint, or hold a familiar object can provide a calming influence and help a child self-regulate.

Your goal is to help the child regulate. Over time, improved behaviors may result. Regardless of the child's behavior, however, know that you have been a voice for God's Word and a living example of His love. God will be at work in that child.

THINK ABOUT

- I can make my classroom a safe place by . . .
- What are some ways I can increase stability and predictability for an emotionally dysregulated child?
- How can I model regulating emotions in the classroom?

You who fear the LORD, trust in the LORD!
He is their help and their shield.
Psalm 115:11

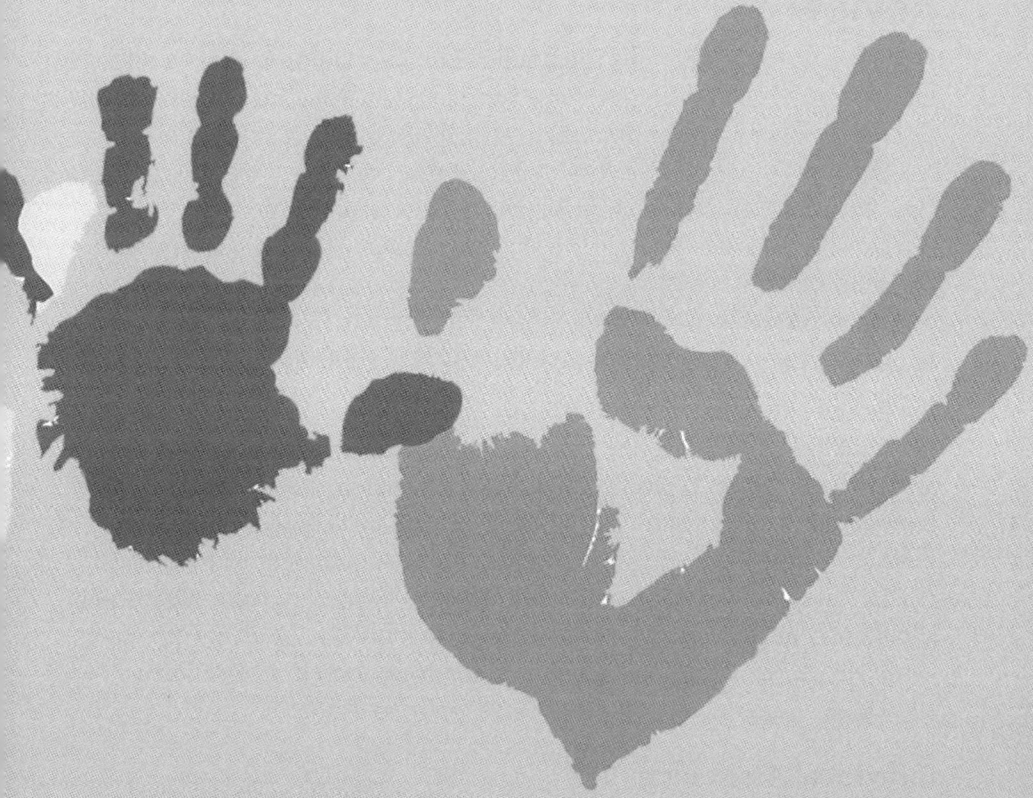

Section 7
Getting Help

OPENING THOUGHT

How could another adult in the classroom help you?

Help!

Lisa Krenz

Review

Have you, the only adult in a room full of bubbling children, ever stood feeling outnumbered and double-teamed and prayed, "Lord, help us all make it through—only forty-four minutes to go"? While prayer is an integral part of teaching, this is not the one you want to be praying every week. Perhaps your class includes Madelyn, who can't manage the scissors for her craft project; Gavin, who reads two levels below the other students; Savannah, who can't communicate her needs and so throws things when she gets overwhelmed; or Carlos, who is very bright and bored with Sunday School and acts up just to make things interesting. It's obvious; you need some help.

Public and parochial schools use terms like paraprofessional, teacher's aide, or individual aide to describe the person you need. In Sunday School, we just ask for a helper. Typically, we think of a helper as someone who provides crowd control and an extra pair of hands. These are certainly valuable commodities, but that helper can be so much more for a student who has specific needs. Have a conversation with your helper to delineate what role he or she should play in your classroom. If you have an individual student with more involved needs, include the parent in this conversation to glean effective strategies.

Individual Assistance

Here are some valuable tasks you might ask a helper to perform.

- Assist with physical needs as appropriate to the child.
- Provide proximity control; an adult presence offers subtle restraining influence.
- Keep the child on task or redirect quietly as needed.
- Adapt worksheets or paper-and-pencil activities as you go along or before class.

- Be a scribe, writing for the student.
- Restate directions or divide tasks into smaller parts for the student.
- Help neighboring students as needed.

For older students, another adult in the room can still provide great benefit.

- Keep the conversation going. When the main teacher asks a question and silence swallows the room, raise a hand, answer the question (whether right or wrong). Keep things moving.
- Facilitate relationships between students.
- Redirect negative behaviors and focus as needed.
- Model faith talk.
- Participate with the students; join in.

Don't be afraid to ask for help. Your whole class will be better off if you don't go it alone.

THINK ABOUT

- A helper in my classroom could . . .
- Mark the listed items above that you would ask your helper to do.
- Which of your students could use individual assistance?

Shall We Dance?

Karen Wittmayer

OPENING THOUGHT

What is the difference between a teacher aide and a team teacher?

Review

The other day I watched a dancing competition and was amazed at the precision and grace with which two bodies can move as one. Team teachers often display some of the same breathtaking skill as—through practice, planning, and prayer—they manage a class of children with differing abilities.

Grouping

Team teachers can divide their class into groups for the entire session or just a portion of it. Use groups when it will support the goal of your lesson or activity. Decide on your groups before the children arrive for class. Benefits include the opportunity to reteach the lesson with a lower student-to-teacher ratio. (During the large-group times, the other teacher is always on duty assisting and redirecting.) Grouping options:

1. Place all children with special needs in the same group. While each teacher presents the same lesson, the techniques vary according to the needs of each group. One group may study the lesson in depth, with details and oral reading. The other teacher may present the lesson in simpler terms, with hands-on activities and much repetition.

2. Spread children with special needs among all groups. The same lessons are taught, with the same materials, utilizing strategies such as peer tutoring and partnering.

Proximity Control

Each week, position one of the teachers near one of the children in your class who has special learning needs. While the lead teacher is presenting the lesson, the other teacher can work directly with that child without drawing undue attention.

Cues

Team teachers benefit from the use of nonverbal signals. In the beginning of the year, brainstorm a few cues. A nod of the head might indicate a student who needs a gentle reminder to sit still or modify behavior; a wink might mean it's time to divide into groups.

Distraction

Sometimes the easiest cure for a restless child is a little time away. One teacher can invite the child to assist with a special project or come along on an errand. The child gets special attention or needed movement and the class is able to continue undistracted.

Team teaching benefits children because teachers are able to teach God's Word in ways that make learning accessible to all children. As you and your partner strive to meet all the educational needs of the children in your class, remember that you are never alone. The Holy Spirit is working through you, and it is God's team on which you serve.

THINK ABOUT

- Team teaching could help me and my students because . . .
- In what situations would it be beneficial to group students based on ability?
- What does the author mean by *proximity control*?

OPENING THOUGHT

Where do you go when you need help with a situation in your classroom?

Help Is Near

Loren Sheppard

Review

When dealing with children who have exceptional learning needs, teachers often feel alone and unsupported. Few volunteer teachers have training for helping students with special needs. Rare is the teacher who doesn't have at least one student who could use extra help. Don't despair! Help is near! Take time to develop relationships with the parents, talented members of your congregation, and other support agencies.

Parents

Parents of children with learning needs quickly become experts in their child's capabilities. If they have concerns about their child being rejected, they may be hesitant to bring him or her to Sunday or midweek school. It is a good strategy to become partners with the parents. Don't hesitate to share both problems and positive experiences that you have in class with them. Invite parents to help find solutions and develop strategies to face the behavior or learning problems you encounter. Remember to approach the situation with a positive statement about the child, asking, "What can we do to help your child learn about God's love?"

Use the talents and experiences of the parents. Invite them to assist in class. If it creates a problem for parents to be in the same class as their child, perhaps they can assist with craft or snack preparation or cleanup. You could also invite them to "trade places" with parents who have a child with similar challenges in another class.

Church Members

Many gifted people belong to every church. For support and counsel, seek out those in your congregation who have expertise with children, especially teachers, psychologists, and educational administrators. Involve artists, business people, and medical professionals to present special lessons. Their special gift may help a child with learning needs understand the message of salvation in Jesus. Male role models are also very important in our church's educational programs.

Not every adult will feel equipped to teach an entire class; invite those who are reluctant to assist you by sitting next to students who need extra help.

Other Agencies

Check out your local school district for resources to help with children that have special learning needs, attention deficit disorder, or other concerns. Those who teach your students in day school classes, especially any special education teachers, will have valuable insights (ask the parents to help you make a connection with these teachers).

In addition, many agencies may have valuable resources for you to use. Consult the list on this page for some specific places of support.

You're not alone. Help is available in many forms. God bless you as you seek the best possible resources for teaching His precious children.

Support Agencies for Special Education

Lutheran Special Education Ministries—www.luthsped.org

Children with Attention Deficit Disorder (CHADD)—www.chadd.org

Learning Disabilities Association of America (LDA)—www.ldaamerica.org

Bethesda Lutheran Communities—www.bethesdalutherancommunities.org

Council for Exceptional Children (CEC)—www.cec.sped.org

THINK ABOUT

- I should share both problems and positive experiences with parents of a child with special needs because . . .
- Which members of your congregation could be valuable resources for your class?
- Why are male role models important in Sunday School?

Let the word of Christ dwell in you richly, teaching and admonishing one another in all wisdom, singing psalms and hymns and spiritual songs, with thankfulness in your hearts to God.
Colossians 3:16

Section 8

Exceptionality and the Arts

OPENING THOUGHT

Do we learn better when we are told something or when we experience it?

The Arts Meet Special Needs

Loren Sheppard

Review

Children with special needs learn best through lessons that use their senses. Seeing, hearing, feeling, and moving reinforces learning. God has blessed us with a world of music, sculpture, drama, and art that depicts the Bible lessons that we teach our children. Effective education can use the arts to allow students to look, touch, and listen—to *experience* the Bible lesson.

Sculpture

Perhaps an artist in your congregation or community is willing to bring some sculpture work to your class. Or perhaps a field trip to a local art museum is possible. After experiencing the work that someone else has created, children with special needs can create their own art to interpret what they have learned in a Bible lesson. For example, they could use clay to sculpt tablets representing the Ten Commandments or make water jars like those used at the wedding in Cana.

Art

The Bible has inspired artists throughout history, and their work is readily available in art books, in museums, and on the Internet. Children can learn details about the Bible account, the story, the customs, and the geography of Bible times by examining paintings of a Bible lesson. After children have observed someone else's work, they can re-create the Bible scenes in their art with watercolors, chalk, or markers. Craft projects can also reinforce the lesson. For example, a child can make the "armor of God" (Ephesians 6:13–17) out of craft supplies or cut apart a picture of that armor to create a puzzle. These kinds of experiences are enjoyable and productive educational activities for a child with learning difficulties.

Music

Children with special needs can experience Bible narratives through Bach cantatas or simple Bible songs. Using music is also an excellent way to memorize Bible verses, the books of the Bible, or simple Bible truths (like "Jesus Loves Me"). You can find excellent teaching songs in the variety of CPH songbooks.

Drama

Watching a stage play is an excellent way to experience a Bible story, but children of all abilities can also learn and have an enjoyable experience by reenacting a Bible event or putting on a play of their own. CPH has several books of dramas for children.

By using the arts, you can create lessons that come alive and give your students an appreciation for the great blessing God has given us throughout history in the work of artists, musicians, and writers.

THINK ABOUT

- Experiencing a lesson is important because . . .
- What could I do to incorporate sculpture, art, music, or drama into my next lesson?
- What could I have my students create that would help them understand Jesus' love?

Music and Special Needs

Lisa Krenz

OPENING THOUGHT

What songs do you remember from childhood?

Review

Scientific research confirms what most of us have known since childhood, whether someone we loved sang to soothe us or we memorized the preamble to the Constitution in song. Music touches both our hearts and our minds. In His infinite wisdom, God designed our brain in such a way that music registers in a different part of the brain than other types of learning and language do. The Lord provided music as an alternate route to understanding and making connections on so many levels.

Music Works on Many Levels

Music is the ideal vehicle to facilitate learning, communication, social interaction, and appropriate behaviors. Music provides a rhythm and predictable structure that may appeal to students with autism, intellectual disabilities, and other learning disabilities. Students who are nonverbal or have limited language skills can participate in music activities using rhythm instruments, hand motions, and actions that interpret the meaning of the lyrics. The use of music is known to help students increase language skills.

Using music as part of the ritual of your classroom facilitates improved behavior as well as provides needed predictability for students. A welcome song sets the tone for the class and signals students that it's time to focus on the teacher. The same is true for specific songs for cleanup, movement, hymn of the day, or closing. If you don't have a song for such occasions, consider using pieces of our standard liturgy, such as "Thank the Lord" (*LSB*, p. 164) or a stanza from "With the Lord Begin Your Task" (*LSB* 869). This will also make students feel more integrated into regular worship. Using liturgy and hymns is also a good musical transition as students get older and don't want to sing "baby" songs anymore.

Of course, it's always good to remember that too much of a good thing is still too much. Be sensitive to students who are easily overstimulated or overwhelmed by loud noises or too much sensory input. Music playing throughout class might cause difficulty for students. Loud banging of instruments might be frightening. Observe your students to determine the kind of music that encourages and the kind of music that overstimulates.

Non-singer Options

I know what you're thinking. "I can't sing." The Bible tells us to make a "joyful noise" unto the Lord. You don't have to be able to sing well to implement music in your classroom. Your students don't expect you to sing like a pop star; they just want to see you enjoying yourself. They will follow your lead. You can play recorded music using speakers and a computer or other device. What you will find is that your students are not the only ones who benefit from the use of music in your classroom. Using music in your classroom will bring you together in a common experience of praising the Lord together. The Holy Spirit will no doubt work wonders in such a teaching and learning situation.

THINK ABOUT

- I could incorporate music into my classroom by . . .
- Make a list of songs that you could use to signal the events of Sunday School (i.e., welcome, cleanup, etc.)?
- How does music help you, the teacher, reach all learners?

OPENING THOUGHT

What is your favorite part about arts and crafts?

The Arts and Crafts Dilemma

Lisa Krenz

Review

A favorite part of the Sunday School lesson is the arts and crafts project. It is a great way to start or end lessons and get children actively involved in the learning process. But have you ever noticed that some students are not enjoying these projects as much as you thought they should? A wide variety of students with exceptional learning needs may struggle with these seemingly wonderful activities.

Be Aware

Children with fine-motor difficulties resulting from cerebral palsy, muscular dystrophy, or brain injury will struggle to punch out, cut, and fold accurately. They may also struggle to color within the lines or control pencils, crayons, and scissors. Children with Down syndrome often have short, thick fingers and poor muscle tone. They may have trouble cutting and writing. In the primary grades, children with learning or developmental disabilities might find it difficult to write their names in small spaces or fill in letters and words. Following complex, multistep directions may also become an issue as the student gets older and projects get more sophisticated. Children with impaired vision might also have problems like these since they may not see well enough to distinguish outlines for coloring or cutting.

Prepare

You don't need to abandon arts and crafts projects. These projects are still a great way to involve children in the lesson and helpful reminders of the lesson for the children to take home, share with their families, and display. But a little extra preparation may be in order to avoid frustration for students with special needs.

Sometimes, the best preparation is just another helper in class—an extra pair of hands to help with cutting and punching out paper and an extra pair of eyes to spot the children who need assistance. Other simple preparations include preparing a model so students can see the finished product, punching out pieces or folding papers before class, providing stickers for decorating, or using washable markers and glue sticks. Check with parents to see if their child uses special scissors or other adaptive tools the Sunday School might duplicate.

For projects that require coloring within boundaries, use puff paint, glitter glue, or yarn on those outlines. This will give the students a tactile clue about where to color and will give them a physical boundary to stop their crayon or marker when they are coloring. This is also helpful for students with vision problems.

Does a child have difficulty writing his or her name? Cut the letters of the name out of sandpaper and glue them to stiff paper. Let the child color over the letters with crayon to make a rubbing of the name. Keep this "signature page" available for future use.

Share Christ

Look over the lesson projects a few days before class and anticipate what will be difficult for your students. This way, if you need to do any gluing or finding special items, you will have time. Keep in mind that the purpose of Sunday School is not to learn how to cut, color, write, or separate perforated pieces of paper. These projects are not an end, but a means to learning about God and His love in Jesus.

THINK ABOUT

- My students sometimes have trouble with arts and crafts because . . .
- How will you use these suggestions to prepare for arts and crafts?
- How do arts and crafts help teach children about God's love?

At that time the disciples came to Jesus, saying, "Who is the greatest in the kingdom of heaven?" And calling to Him a child, He put him in the midst of them and said, "Truly, I say to you, unless you turn and become like children, you will never enter the kingdom of heaven. Whoever humbles himself like this child is the greatest in the kingdom of heaven. Whoever receives one such child in My name receives Me." Matthew 18:1–5

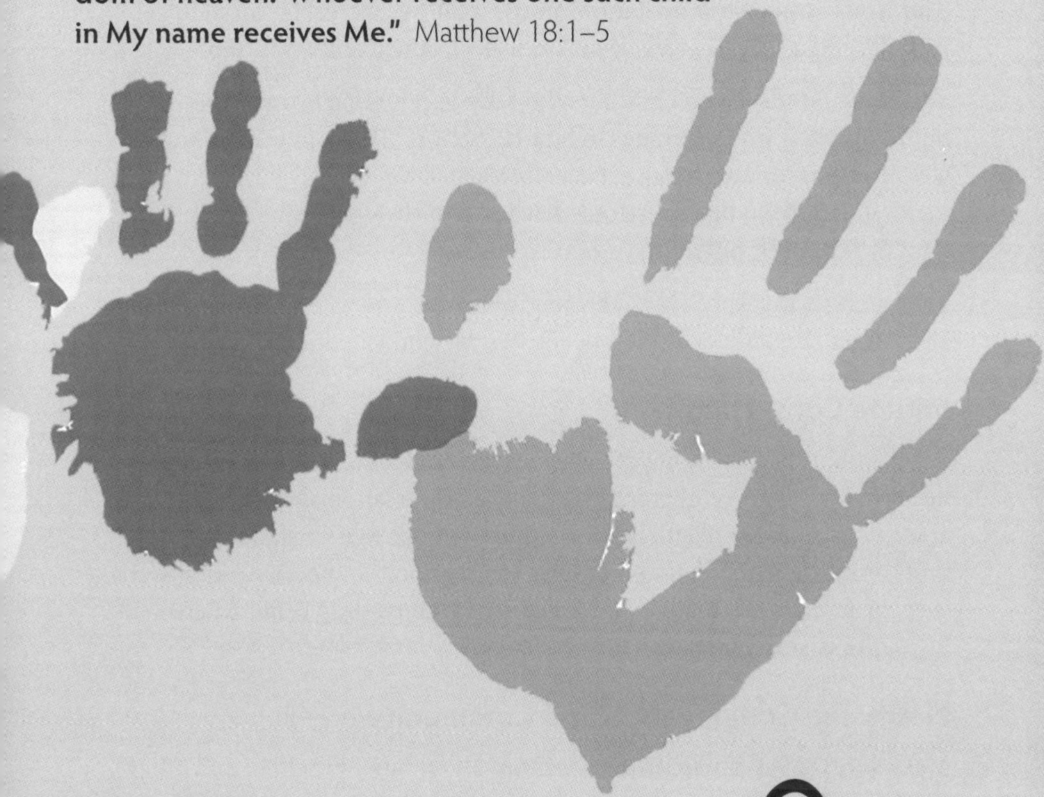

Section 9

Reinventing Attitudes

OPENING THOUGHT

Think of an invitation you got that made you feel special.

I-N-V-I-T-E Someone

Lisa Krenz

Review

Kids love getting party invitations in the mail. We all feel honored to get an invitation to a special event. It makes us feel valued and important.

Too often, families with children who have exceptional learning needs do not feel invited when it comes to Sunday School. They know *everybody* is welcome, but they aren't sure if *everybody* includes their child. There are so many situations in life where they have had to struggle for inclusion. Will Sunday School be different?

The letters in the word INVITE can give us some ideas for making sure that all children, regardless of their needs, feel welcome in Sunday School.

Initiate Conversation

When you notice a parent with a Sunday School–aged child with special needs in church, greet them and initiate a conversation about Sunday School. "I see your child is old enough for Sunday School. We would love to have him (or her) attend." You do not have to mention the special need. Just make sure the family feels invited and welcome. It seems simple, but a personal invitation is very powerful.

Notify the Congregation and Community

Make sure that all publicity that goes out about Sunday School and other Christian education opportunities indicates that all children are welcome, including children with special needs.

Visit

Arrange a brief visit to get to know the parents and the child a little better. Address the specific needs of the child. Bring some sample Sunday School lessons. Talk about the best way to adapt lessons for that student. Give the parents and child an opportunity to ask questions or express concerns about Sunday School.

Include All Children

Make sure that your lessons include all children in your classroom and allow their full participation. Anticipate their needs, and plan for them.

Tell about Jesus

From your first conversation with a family to your weekly lessons, make sharing the love of Jesus your primary focus.

Enjoy

Enjoy the mixture of children in your class and the individual gifts of each child. The Lord will surely bless your class with His joy. "Whoever receives one such child in My name receives Me" (Matthew 18:5).

THINK ABOUT

- I can initiate conversation with new families by . . .
- How can your church clearly indicate that all children are welcome in Sunday School?
- During your initial visit, what information do you need to exchange with the parents of a child with special needs?

OPENING THOUGHT

How do you make a new friend?

Talking to Children about People with Disabilities

Lisa Krenz

Review

We often believe young children to be very accepting of those who are different, not yet troubled by prejudices or negative stereotypes. Even if this is true—and it is not always the case—children will still have questions about classmates who have obvious disabilities or special needs. You should start with the basics, allowing no child to be teased and maintaining a personal accepting attitude that will be contagious. Respecting one another should be the standard of behavior in your classroom.

You can go a long way in easing the entry of a new student with special needs by having a discussion with the class before the new student's arrival.

Some Discussion Points

- What do you do when you make a new friend?
- What are some things you and your friends like to do at recess?
- How are you the same as your friends? What do you have in common?
- How are you different from your friends?
- Does God love you because you're really good at something, like basketball or reading? (No)
- Does God love each of you the same? (Yes)
- We all have different gifts. No matter how fast we can read or do math or speak, God has given us gifts. What are some of our new friend's gifts?

Answer questions honestly but in simple terms that children can understand. They may ask why a person is in a wheelchair or doesn't speak intelligibly. Never make up an answer. If you don't know, tell them that you don't know.

Some Ways to Say Things

- The connection between her brain and her legs doesn't work right, so her legs don't get the message to stand.
- He doesn't learn to read and write as fast as some other kids, but he is smart in other ways.
- At school she has a special teacher because she learns things in a different way.
- No, you can't "catch it" from playing together.
- He can understand you. He just can't speak a message back as easily as you can.
- Some people have an intellectual disability, which means they don't learn as fast or as much as other people—but their hearts can love just as much as other people.
- People with an intellectual disability were sometimes called "mentally retarded." Now, some people use the word *retarded* in a mean way. We will never use it in that way. In music, the word *ritard* means to play something more slowly and more beautifully. That's how we will think of that word.
- Sometimes he makes strange noises or startles easily. He doesn't mean to scare you—it's just the way he reacts when he's nervous, excited, or happy.

THINK ABOUT

- How can you foster a personal attitude of acceptance?
- How would you start a conversation about a new classmate with special needs?
- If a student teased another student because of a disability, I would . . .

OPENING THOUGHT

Why is it important to have a positive attitude about something new?

Reinventing Attitudes

Karen Wittmayer

Review

You know you'll have a student next year with exceptional learning needs. You wonder if you're up to the challenge. You're not alone. Sunday School children with special needs are almost always placed with their same-aged peers. Sometimes we as Sunday School teachers are called upon to reinvent our attitudes about having children with special needs in our classes.

A Two-Step Process

The first and most important step is prayer and reliance on the promises of God: "I can do all things through [Christ] who strengthens me" (Philippians 4:13); "Set your minds on things that are above, not on things that are on earth" (Colossians 3:2); "Whatever is true, whatever is honorable, whatever is just, whatever is pure, whatever is lovely, whatever is commendable, if there is any excellence, if there is anything worthy of praise, think about these things" (Philippians 4:8).

The second step is to simply take action. You can reinvent your attitude in several ways.

- **Plan for this student.** Consider seating—up front by you or in the rear where there is extra wiggle room? Prepare a class discipline plan so the child knows exactly what you expect, and then reward her for even close approximations. Pick easier reading selections for that student and shorter memory verses. Always ask, "How can I reach *all* my students this week?"
- **Ask for extra helpers.** A volunteer can be a special friend to this child. It's great if the special friend can be consistent each week, but it's not necessary. This friend acts to redirect the student's attention, whispers gentle reminders of behavior expectations, and gives one-on-one help with activities that may be difficult for the student.

- **Talk to the child's parents** about any "tips or tricks" that might be helpful. Ask for permission to talk with the child's Day School teacher about learning strategies that work.
- **Research.** Talk to education or special education professionals in your congregation. Search the Web. There are many Web sites that provide easy-to-read, useful information for volunteer teachers.

Repeat the Message

They say that for a belief pattern or attitude to be reinvented, the new thought must be heard 21 times! In order for a child to change his thought of "I'm not wanted here" to "My teacher likes me," he must hear it 21 times. In order for you to reinvent your attitude about having this child in class, you can remind yourself in many times, places, and situations why you're glad he or she is in your class. No wonder the Bible tells us to think on these things!

THINK ABOUT

- I can show my students I like them and want them in Sunday School by . . .
- How can you reach all of your students next week?
- What else does God promise you in this situation?

OPENING THOUGHT

What can your congregation do to better welcome people of all abilities?

Let the Children Come

Anita Reith Stohs

Review

What can a congregation do to include children with disabilities into the church? We know that each child is part of the family of God to which we have all been called through Baptism. All of us need the power of the Spirit to transform us into a new creation in Christ. Jesus wants all children to come to Him, whatever their ability or disability. His love is inclusive, as should be ours.

Early Welcome

The first thing a congregation can do to welcome a child with disabilities is to show love and acceptance from the very beginning of their life. When the child is born, welcome the new baby just like you would welcome any other child and assist the new parents in any way possible. Understand that parents who have a newborn with disabilities face even greater pressures than the average new parents. I experienced this pressure firsthand when my daughter was born with a disability.

Encourage new parents of a child with a disability to bring their baby to church. Children with developmental disabilities go through the stages of childhood at a slower pace, and they often may not demonstrate age-appropriate behavior. Help congregational members be understanding when this is the case. Certain disabilities lead to disruptive outbursts. Prepare congregational members by mentioning this possibility and encourage them to be prepared and understanding when this occurs.

Starting Sunday School

When a child with a disability prepares to attend your Sunday School or midweek program, share information about the child's specific disability with the teaching staff, as well as the students in the classroom. The child's parents may be your best source of information, though a church member who teaches special education might be useful to help explain good special education teaching techniques. Most often children with special needs just want someone to show them love, which they often show freely to anyone.

Encourage your congregational Board of Education to also become better informed about the needs of children with disabilities, and to seek ways in which they can lead your congregation to reach out to an often unchurched group of children and parents in your community.

As much as possible, allow children with disabilities to attend church programs with other children. Many children with disabilities go to early public school preschool programs, and they are familiar with group settings. If needed, recruit an aide to assist the teacher, providing help not just for the child with the disability, but for other students too.

While inclusion is most workable in the early years; as a child with a disability gets older, the mental distance between them and their same-aged classmates increases. Consider an alternative approach at this point. One option is to allow children with disabilities to be in a class with one another, which allows for teaching more at their level of understanding.

Confirmation Years

When it was time for confirmation, we combined our daughter with a girl from a neighboring congregation to form a special instruction class.

A major challenge is what to do with children with disabilities after confirmation. Few churches have programs aimed at this population. Whenever possible, include these young teens in youth group activities that are appropriate, as well in general church functions. Servant activities offer additional options for involvement, depending upon the level of disability. Adults with Down syndrome can be excellent greeters, and they can help with meals or yard work. Last year, when one of my sons was teaching in Austria, he reported seeing adults with Down syndrome help with ushering and taking the collection at a church he attended—the church had a program for adults with developmental disabilities, and it incorporated these adults into the life of their church.

Gifts to Share

I have discovered over the years that children with disabilities have their own gifts to share with the church. They are often more able than the rest of us to show love to others. Hearing a group of children with disabilities welcome fellow classmates into their room is a demonstration of unconditional acceptance that the rest of us would do well to emulate.

When my daughter was five, she attended two half-day preschools each school day: one at a public school and the other at a church. At that time, the public school teacher commented that my daughter was positively affecting the other children in her class. Over the years, I have come to better understand what this teacher meant. An acquaintance recently described his brother with Down syndrome this way: "My brother taught me to see that I was not the center of the universe; from him I learned to be more compassionate towards others." I hear similar comments from other individuals who have volunteered the information of how an early, positive experience with a child with a disability affected their later choice of vocation. The distinction between student and teacher blurs when you include children with disabilities into your classroom.

My daughter and her friends have the faith of a child. They have a trust in their Savior unencumbered by the cares of this world. "Let the children come to Me," says our Savior. May we follow our Lord in encouraging all children, of all ability levels, to find a place within the family of God.

THINK ABOUT

- When Jesus said, "Let the children come," He meant . . .
- Does your church fully include students with disabilities in Sunday School classes with their peers?
- What gifts do the students in your class have to share?